SousVide Supreme

the cookbook

edited by Mary Dan Eades

photography by Mehosh Dziadzio

Paradox Press

contents

introduction

Though elite chefs in multi-star restaurants have relied on the sous vide technique to cook fabulous food for decades—it's what enables them to reliably produce exquisite dishes time after time for scores of diners—the trend to move this "culinary secret" out of the restaurant kitchen and onto the kitchen counter top is a fairly recent phenomenon. But in a short space of time, legions of cooks, from the foodie/gourmet cook to the busy mom or dad, have eagerly embraced sous vide cooking as a means to create amazing food themselves at home at the touch of a button.

The sous vide technique is a different way of cooking. Food is vacuum sealed in cooking-safe pouches and submerged in a water bath held at a precisely-controlled temperature. In contrast to traditional cooking methods that rely on the perfect timing of food being cooked at aggressively high temperatures (such as a 400°F/ 200°C oven, griddle, or grill), sous vide cooking relies on perfect precision in temperature control, and time takes a back seat. With the sous vide method, food cooks gently, at its ideal serving temperature, so it can't overcook or dry out, even if left in the water bath significantly longer than needed to reach serving temperature. The end result? Perfectly cooked, more nutritious food!

Why more nutritious? The sealed cooking pouch locks in flavor and nutrition. Water soluble vitamins and healthful antioxidants, which are present in the colorful skins of fruits and vegetables, remain with the food in the pouch instead of being lost to cooking liquid or steam. The vacuum pouch and gentle temperatures protect the delicate fats in fish, seafood, and meat that would be turned from something healthful to something harmful by exposure to oxygen and high heat in traditional cooking. Pre-cooking foods for barbecue sous vide, then quickly searing, limits the production of potential cancer-causing chemicals from charring on the grill.

In this book, you'll learn all the basics of sous vide cooking that will make it easy to elevate the ordinary to the extraordinary. You'll find complete time and temperature charts for all types of foods and food prep and safety information, along with the how-to instructions for many useful (and really simple) techniques, such as quick chilling and sealing with the displacement method. Anyone—from a good home cook, foodie, or DIY chef to a complete kitchen novice—can turn out: meat cooked perfectly edge to edge; moist, delicate fish and seafood; chicken breasts that are never dried out and tough or undercooked; ribs with meat that literally falls off the bone. All with minimal hands on time and at the push of a button, every time!

This book puts 100+ kitchen-tested recipes for easy-to-prepare sous vide dishes at your fingertips for everything from beef, poultry, lamb, pork, game, fish, seafood, vegetables, and side dishes to starters, cocktails and desserts! If you are looking for something very basic, try Rainy Day Rib-eye Steak, Lemon and Paprika Salmon, Corn on the Cob, or Risotto with Ham and Mushrooms. In the mood for the exotic? Lamb Belly with Turkish Spice, Chicken Afrique, even Octopus, Relish and Corn Pudding will fill that bill. Something gourmet? Check out the Proscuitto-wrapped Rabbit Saddle, Fennel-scented Cornish Game Hen, or Stuffed Quail with Goat Cheese Grits. And don't forget the sweet treats: Chocolate Zabaglione, Masala Chai Crème Brûlée, Dulce de Leche, and more!

The recipes in this cookbook come to us from a variety of worldwide sources, from award-winning chefs to foodie bloggers, celebrity chefs and bartenders, and our own anonymous staff of culinary specialists. You'll find those contributed by our chef/bartender ambassadors and blogosphere foodies credited with their names, but you'll also find more information about each of them in the contributor bios on page 206. They have all been of immeasurable help in building a global community of food-loving, sous vide fans, and we gratefully acknowledge their help.

~ *Mary Dan Eades, Editor*
Director of Culinary Operations, SousVide Supreme

sous vide basics

Cooking sous vide (a French term meaning under vacuum) involves vacuum-sealing a given food—meat, fish, poultry, vegetables, fruit—in a cooking pouch and submerging it in a temperature-controlled water bath for as long as it takes to bring the food to the desired temperature throughout. Food cooks gently and precisely and cannot overcook, since it can only reach the temperature of the water in the bath. Flavor and moisture that would normally escape into the air or drip into the pan stay locked in the food pouch, which produces the most flavorful, tender, and juicy food possible.

Chef George Pralus developed the technique in France about 40 years ago as a method for perfectly cooking and minimizing the costly shrinkage of foie gras. Chef Bruno Goussalt popularized the technique by introducing it in the first-class cabin cuisine on Air France's international flights. Since then, it has become a favored cooking technique of great chefs around the globe, and the secret weapon of chefs in competitions.

The introduction in 2009 of the SousVide Supreme,™ the first water oven designed for kitchen counter tops, made the technique practical for everyone, from the rank novice to the accomplished cook.

How does sous vide cooking work?

Unlike traditional cooking methods, such as roasting, broiling, grilling, or sautéing, that use aggressively high temperatures to heat the air around the food, the sous vide technique relies on the superior ability of water to transfer heat to food. Because the transfer of heat through water is many times faster than the transfer of heat through air, removing all, or at least most, of the air from the cooking pouch—creating the vacuum seal—is important, as pockets of air between the pouch and the food can result in uneven cooking.

When cooking sous vide, the water bath temperature is set at precisely the desired target for doneness—for instance, 146°F (63.5°C) for perfectly done chicken breasts. Foods cook gently for (at a minimum) long enough to allow the heat of the water to penetrate to the center of the food. How long that process takes has been carefully worked out mathematically for a wide variety of food types, and depends not as much on the weight of the food being cooked as on its thickness. For example, if it takes 40 minutes to bring a piece of chicken that is one-inch thick to temperature, it might take two-and-a-half hours to bring a two-inch thick piece to that temperature. It is important, for food safety, to carefully adhere to the minimum cooking times and holding instructions.

The simple steps of sous vide cooking

1. Season your food lightly with salt and pepper, or fresh or dried herbs and spices.

2. Seal the food in an appropriately-sized food-grade cooking pouch. There are several types of cooking pouches and sealing methods. A chamber vacuum sealer will seal both solids and liquids in cooking pouches, as well as in a variety of storage containers. A suction sealer may be used to seal pouches containing less than a tablespoon of liquid; and zip-seal cooking pouches provide a convenient and inexpensive way to seal liquid-rich foods (see page 11). By simply lowering the filled, unsealed zip pouch into the water bath, the air is displaced by the water, and the zip-closure can be sealed when it reaches the surface.

3. Simmer the food at the desired temperature in the preheated water bath for at least the minimum recommended amount of time to ensure it is heated to the center. In most cases, you can leave the food in the water bath substantially longer without loss of quality.

4. Sear or sauce your food, if desired. All foods that have been cooked sous vide will be delicious straight from the pouch; but some benefit from a complementary sauce or a quick sear in a hot skillet, on a grill, or with a kitchen torch to impart the expected crisp, golden crust.

Tips for sous vide cooking

Plan your menu in advance. Cook foods that need some time (spare ribs, short ribs, flank steak, pork roast, pork belly, and tough or grass fed cuts) over night or even a couple of days. Quick-chill them thoroughly (see page 12) and refrigerate. Then cook foods that take the shortest amount of time.

Group foods together according to the temperatures that they cook. Red meats (beef, lamb) can all cook at the same temperature to your preferred degree of doneness: rare, medium-rare, medium, or medium-well. White meats (chicken or turkey breast) and pork (chops, ribs, or roasts) can cook at the same temperature. Turkey or duck thighs and legs cook hotter—176°F (80°C)—and longer, so they're a breeze to do overnight. Fruits and vegetables of every type can cook at the same temperature—in the range of 180°F (82°C) to 185°F (85°C)—in about 30 minutes to an hour-and-a-half, depending on their size and tenderness or toughness.

The length of cooking required depends on two things: thickness of the food in the pouch and its tenderness or toughness. Tender cuts merely need to be brought to the desired temperature—perhaps 45 minutes to an hour for a 1-inch piece of steak—then finished with a quick sear. Though they may be heated through in the same hour, long, slow cooking of short ribs (48 hours) or lamb belly (36 hours) allows their plentiful collagen to gelatinize and melt, giving them succulence and transforming their toughness into pull-apart tenderness.

sealing liquids

Preparing liquid-rich foods for sous vide cooking can be accomplished using a chamber vacuum sealer, or by evacuating most of the air in a zip-closure cooking pouch so it will stay submerged in the water bath. The displacement method for evacuating air is based on a principle first stated in the second century BCE by Greek physicist and mathematician Archimedes: *Any object, wholly or partially immersed in fluid, is buoyed up by a force equal to the weight of the fluid displaced by the object.*

Using zip-closure cooking pouches

Zip-closure cooking pouches make it easy to cook sous vide sauces, syrups, glazes, infusions, ice cream bases, soups, stews, braises, and more. Here are the simple steps to sealing them for sous vide cooking:

1 Lower the filled pouch, with the zipper still open, into the water bath, or a large pot of cooler water, if preferred. The weight of the water will press against the sides of the pouch and force the air out

2 Once the zip closure is at the surface, zip it closed.

3 Submerge the sealed pouch in the water bath for cooking.

food safety

As with all cooking methods, it is important to use clean, fresh ingredients and to work with clean hands and tools on clean surfaces. When cooking food sous vide for immediate consumption—what is termed *Cook-Serve*—the basic rules of food handling will suffice, because the food will remain hot in the machine until serving and will sometimes get a final high-temperature sear.

On occasion, especially when entertaining, it is helpful to employ a technique, used widely by restaurant chefs, called *Cook-Chill-Hold*. In this method, food is vacuum-sealed and cooked to completion in the water oven in advance, and then quick-chilled in an ice water bath for long enough to return it to refrigerator temperature, and out of the so-called "danger zone." The danger zone is the temperature range between 40°F (5°C) and 130°F (54°C) where food-borne bacteria can grow most easily. Even though most of the potentially harmful bacteria will be killed by sous vide cooking, some can protect themselves from the heat by hibernating as dormant forms—called *spores*—that can blossom again given sufficient time and favorable temperatures.

To reduce the risk of food-borne illness when using the Cook-Chill-Hold method, follow these important guidelines:

• Quick-chill the warm cooking pouches of food fully submerged in an ice water bath (half ice and half water) for long enough to ensure a quick drop back to refrigerated temperature. Generally this will be the same length as the minimum time required to bring the food to temperature. Add ice as needed.

• Immediately after chilling either refrigerate or freeze in the pouch.

• Hold refrigerated pouches of sous vide cooked food for no more than 48 hours; properly frozen food pouches should remain safe for up to one year.

• To ensure safety in holding, particularly with home refrigerators, be sure the refrigerator compartment maintains a temperature below 40°F (5°C), and that the freezer maintains a temperature below 0°F (-17°C).

measuring ingredients

Because of the precisely controlled temperatures used in sous vide cooking, recipes can be reproduced perfectly time after time. But as with any culinary technique, the success of the recipe also depends on correctly measured ingredients. Different ingredients are measured in different ways and, depending on where you live, using different measuring utensils. In order to ensure that our recipes can be successfully prepared by everyone—whether you live in Des Moines or Tokyo—the ingredient amounts have been specified using both volume and mass (weight).

Volume measurements

Mass equivalencies for US volume measuring spoons (teaspoons and tablespoons) are given as UK metric measuring spoons (milliliters). The same metric amounts are equivalent to gram measuring spoons, which are common in Asia. The volume measure conversions based on cooking spoons are:

> ¼ teaspoon = 1.25 ml spoon
>
> ½ teaspoon = 2.5 ml spoon
>
> 1 teaspoon = 5 ml spoon
>
> 1 tablespoon = 15 ml spoon

For liquids, the volume measure conversions based on cooking utensils are:

> 1 cup = 8 oz = 240 ml

Dry volume measures, as well as fluid measurements greater than 1 cup volume, have been converted to actual weights. For example, 1 cup of crumbled Feta cheese weighs 5 oz/150 g, while 1 cup of fine cornmeal weighs 6.3 oz/186 g. A pint of liquid is accurately converted to 16 oz/473 ml, not estimated based on 240 ml per cup.

temperatures and times

Sous vide cooking is about bringing a given food gently to its perfectly cooked temperature. But perfection, to a degree, lies in the taste of the beholder. One cook's perfect medium-rare steak is found unerringly at 134°F (56.5°C), while another's might be a few degrees higher or lower. That's the beauty of the precision of sous vide cooking! Once you have determined what perfection means to you, whether for meat, fish, poultry, game, fruits, or vegetables, you can dial it in every time precisely to your liking.

Time is a little less subjective, however, at least on the minimum side of things. The amount of time that it takes a pouch of food to be brought to temperature throughout is a function of its thickness, or more precisely, the distance the heat of the water bath must travel to reach the center of the food. Fortunately, the time required for the heat to make that journey can be determined with mathematical precision. And more fortunately still, for those of us not able or willing to pull out the pencil and calculator, the grunt work has been done for us by diligent mathematicians, such as Dr. Douglas Baldwin, and all put neatly into tabular form.

Time also tenderizes, which can be of great benefit to tougher cuts of meat. Tender foods, however, can lose some textural quality if left too long. Thus, you'll also often find a range of time from the minimum required to a maximum recommended time in many recipes and in our cooking charts.

You'll notice that we've given recommended temperatures and recommended minimum and maximum times in the tables on the following pages. These are safe, reliable touch points that should please most people's tastes. They are a good reference from which to begin your sous vide cooking journey. You may also notice that, in some cases, the instructions given in our recipes may not always precisely agree with the recommended times and temperatures in the tables. These discrepancies occur because the temperatures and times in a given recipe are those of the author of that particular recipe—the chef or cook who developed it. It's the way they did it and the way they like it. You may find that you prefer a given food cooked a little hotter or cooler or longer or less, and that's up to you. Dialing in perfection as you see it and being able to repeat it time and again is a part of the beauty of sous vide cooking.

doneness target temperatures

FOOD	DONENESS	TEMPERATURE	
		°F	°C
BEEF, VEAL, LAMB, GAME	Rare	120	49
	Medium Rare	134	56.5
	Medium	140	60
	Medium Well	150	65.5
	Well Done	160 and over	71 and over
PORK	Medium Rare	134	56.5
	Medium	140	60
	Well Done	160 and over	71 and over
POULTRY, White Meat	Medium	140-146	60-63
DUCK, White Meat	Medium Rare	134	56.5
POULTRY, Dark Meat	Well Done	176	80
FISH, SEAFOOD	Rare	116	47
	Medium Rare	126	52
	Medium	140	60
VEGETABLES, FRUITS	—	183-190	84-87
EGGS	soft cooked	147 or 167	64 or 75
	hard cooked	160	71
	scrambled	167	75
	pasteurized	135	57

△ *CAUTION*

Raw or unpasteurized food must never be consumed by immune compromised or highly susceptible individuals. The United States Food Code recommends that, for safety, food should not be kept between 41°F (5°C) and 130°F (54.5°C) for longer than four hours.

recommended cooking temperatures and times

FOOD	THICKNESS[1]		TEMPERATURE		TIME	
	inch	cm	°F	°C	min	max
BEEF, VEAL, LAMB, GAME						
Tender Cuts	1	2.5	134 or higher	56.5 or higher	1 hr	4 hrs
Tenderloin, Rib-eye, T-bone, Chops, Cutlets	2	5	134 or higher	56.5 or higher	3 hrs	6 hours
Tough Cuts and Grassfed[2]						
Bison, Game	1	2.5	134 or higher	56.5 or higher	8-10 hrs	12-24 hrs
Lamb Roast or Leg	2.75	7	134 or higher	56.5 or higher	10 hrs	24-48 hrs
Spare Ribs	2	5	134 or higher	56.5 or higher	24 hrs	48-72 hrs
Flank Steak, Brisket	1	2.5	134 or higher	56.5 or higher	8 hrs	24 hrs
	2	5	134 or higher	56.5 or higher	12 hrs	30 hrs
PORK						
Tenderloin	1.5	4	134 or higher	56.5 or higher	90 min	6-8 hrs
Baby Back Ribs			165	74	4-8 hrs	24 hrs
Chops, Cutlets	1	2.5	134 or higher	56.5 or higher	2-4 hrs	6-8 hrs
	2	5	134 or higher	56.5 or higher	4-6 hrs	8-10 hrs
Roast	2.75	7	160-176	71-80	12 hrs	30 hrs
Spare Ribs	2.75	7	160-176	71-80	12 hrs	30 hrs
Belly (quick)	2	5	185	85	5 hrs	8 hrs
Belly (slow)	2	5	167	75	24 hrs	48-72 hrs
POULTRY						
White Meat						
Chicken Breast, bone in	2	5	146 or higher	63.5 or higher	2.5 hrs	4-6 hrs
Chicken Breast, boneless	1	2.5	146 or higher	63.5 or higher	1 hr	2-4 hrs
Turkey Breast, bone in	2.75	7	146 or higher	63.5 or higher	4 hrs	6-8 hrs
Turkey Breast, boneless	2	5	146 or higher	63.5 or higher	2.5 hrs	4-6 hrs
Duck Breast	1	2.5	134 or higher	63.5 or higher	90 min	4-6 hrs
Dark Meat						
Chicken Leg or Thigh, bone in			165-176	74-80	4 hrs	6-8 hrs
Chicken Thigh, boneless	1	2.5	165-176	74-80	2 hrs	4-6 hrs
Turkey Leg or Thigh			165-176	74-80	8 hrs	10 hrs
Duck Leg			165-176	74-80	8 hrs	18 hrs
Split Game Hen	2.75	7	150 or higher	65.5 or higher	6 hrs	8 hrs

[1] Thickness measurements are based on the thickest section of the food and measured through the vacuum-sealed pouch. Cooking times are for foods starting at refrigerator temperature. Add 15 minutes if starting from frozen.

[2] Tough cuts of meat will heat through to serving temperature in the same time as tender cuts. We recommend longer cooking times for lean, tough cuts to tenderize them.

recommended cooking temperatures and times

FOOD	THICKNESS[1]		TEMPERATURE		TIME	
	inch	cm	°F	°C	min	max
SEAFOOD						
Fish	0.5 - 1	1.25 - 2.5	126 or higher	52 or higher	20 min	30 min
Tuna, Halibut, Snapper, Sole, Salmon, Trout, Mackerel	1 - 2	2.5 - 5	126 or higher	52 or higher	30 min	40 min
Crustaceans, Mollusks						
Lobster	1	2.5	140	60	45 min	60 min
Scallops	1	2.5	140	60	40 min	60 min
Shrimp	jumbo	jumbo	140	60	30 min	40 min
VEGETABLES						
Root	up to 1	up to 2.5	183	84	1-2 hrs	4 hrs
Carrots, Parsnips, Potato, Turnips, Celery Root, Beets	1 - 2	2.5 - 5	183	84	2.5 hrs	4 hrs
Tender Asparagus, Broccoli, Corn, Cauliflower, Eggplant, Onions, Green Beans, Fennel, Squash, Fresh Peas	up to 1	up to 2.5	183	84	30 min	1.5 hrs
FRUIT						
Firm Apple, Pear	up to 1	up to 2.5	183	84	45 min	2 hrs
Soft Peach, Apricot, Plum, Mango, Papaya, Nectarine, Berries	up to 1	up to 2.5	183	84	30 min	1 hr
EGGS[3]						
Soft-cooked in shell (quick)	large	large	167	75	15 min	18 min
Soft-cooked in shell (slow)	large	large	146	63.5	45 min	1.5 hrs
Hard-cooked in shell	large	large	160	71	45 min	1.5 hrs
Pasteurized in shell	large	large	135	57	1.25 hrs	2 hrs
Scrambled (5 eggs)	large	large	167	75	20 min	20 min

[3] Eggs cooked in the shell should not be sealed in cooking pouches.

sous vide egg video
scan the code with your smart phone,
or visit sousvidesupreme.com/thecookbook

cocktails

lychee vodka 21

mango lychee martini 21

Earl Grey gin 22

Earl Grey marteani 22

kümmel 23

Kingston cocktail 23

red pepper rum and ginger syrup 25

red rum daisy 25

raspberry syrup 27

Clover Club cocktail 27

falernum 29

new frisco cocktail 29

rum shrub 30

sunrise cocktail 30

peach brandy 31

fish house punch 31

pineapple syrup 33

Pisco punch 33

lychee vodka

15 lychee nuts, canned

1 bottle (25 oz/750 ml) vodka
(or grain spirits)

3 cups (24 oz/710 ml)
simple syrup

mango lychee martini

Ice cubes

1½ ounces (45 ml) lychee vodka

1 ounce (30 ml) fresh mango purée*

1 drop Blue Curaçao

1 ounce (60 ml) lemonade

1 ounce (60 ml) water

1 slice fresh mango, for garnish

** To make mango purée, peel and
cut into chunks a soft, ripe mango (or
use frozen, thawed mango). Purée in
a blender with a little water to a thick,
but pourable, consistency.*

Courtesy of Ivaylo Peshev

Makes 1.5 liters
Cooking time: 1 hour

1. Fill and preheat the water oven to 153°F (57°C).

2. Put the lychees and vodka into a large (1 gallon/3.8 liter) zip-closure cooking pouch. Evacuate the air (page 11) and seal.

3. Submerge the pouch in the water oven and cook for 1 hour.

4. Remove the pouch and submerge it in an ice water bath (half ice, half water) for 20 to 30 minutes to quick-chill the contents.

5. Strain the infused vodka through a fine mesh sieve into a large bowl and discard the solids.

6. Add the simple syrup to the vodka, and mix well.

7. Pour into two or more clean bottles, label, date, and store, tightly-capped, in the refrigerator for up to six weeks.

mango lychee martini

1. In a cocktail shaker with ice, combine all ingredients, except garnish, and shake well to chill.

2. Strain into a martini glass.

3. Garnish with a slice of fresh mango.

Earl Grey gin

4 tablespoons (60 ml) loose leaf Earl Grey tea

1 bottle (25 oz/750 ml) gin

Earl Grey marteani

1 tablespoon (15 ml) granulated sugar, for rimming glass

1 wedge lemon

Ice cubes

2 ounces (60 ml) Earl Grey gin

1 ounce (30 ml) fresh lemon juice

1 ounce (30 ml) simple syrup

Lemon twist, for garnish

Courtesy of Chef Brian McCracken and Chef Dana Tough

Makes 750 ml
Cooking time: 7 minutes

1. Fill and preheat the water oven to 135°F (57°C).

2. Put the tea and gin into a large (1 gallon/3.8 liter) zip-closure cooking pouch, evacuate the air (page 11) and seal.

3. Submerge the pouch in the water oven and cook for 7 minutes. Longer cooking times will cause the infusion to become bitter. You only want to extract the floral notes of the tea, not its bitterness.

4. Transfer the pouch immediately to an ice water bath (half ice, half water), and quick chill for 10 minutes.

5. Strain the mixture through a fine mesh sieve into a clean bottle immediately after cooling.

6. Store, tightly-capped, in the refrigerator for up to six weeks.

Earl Grey marteani

Courtesy of Nathan Weber

Makes 1 cocktail

1. Pour the sugar onto a small, shallow plate.

2. Moisten the rim of a cocktail or martini glass with a wedge of lemon, dip the moistened rim into the sugar, and set aside.

3. Put ice cubes into a cocktail shaker, pour in the Earl Grey gin, lemon juice, and simple syrup, cover, and shake until the outside of the shaker has frosted.

4. Strain into the rimmed glass, garnish with the lemon wedge or a twist, and serve.

kümmel

2 teaspoons (10 ml) caraway seeds
4 cups (32 oz/946 ml)
simple syrup
1 cup (8 oz/240 ml) vodka

Kingston cocktail
Ice cubes
$1^1/_2$ ounces (45 ml) Jamaican rum
1 ounce (30 ml) orange juice
$^1/_2$ ounce (15 ml) kümmel
$^1/_4$ ounce (7.5 ml) Pimento Dram
Orange twist, for garnish

Courtesy of Chef Brian McCracken and Chef Dana Tough

Makes 1.2 liters
Cooking time: 2 hours

1. Fill and preheat the water oven to 135°F (57°C).

2. Put the caraway seeds, simple syrup and vodka into a large
(1 gallon/3.8 liter) zip-closure cooking pouch, evacuate the air
(page 11) and seal.

3. Submerge the pouch in the water oven and cook for 2 hours.

4. Remove the pouch and submerge it in an ice water bath (half ice,
half water) for 20 to 30 minutes to quick-chill the contents.

5. Strain the mixture through a fine mesh sieve into a clean bottle and
discard the solids.

6. Store, tightly capped, labeled and dated, in the refrigerator for up
to six weeks.

Kingston cocktail

Makes 1 cocktail

1. In a cocktail shaker, over ice cubes, add all ingredients, except garnish, and shake well to chill.

2. Pour into a stemmed cocktail or coupe glass* and garnish with the twist.

* A coupe glass is a shallow, broad-bowled, stemmed glass customarily used for champagne.

red pepper rum and ginger syrup

Courtesy of Chef Brian McCracken and Chef Dana Tough

Makes 750 ml of rum and 1.2 liters of syrup
Cooking time: 3 hours

1. Fill and preheat the water oven to 135°F (57°C).

2. Core and slice the red peppers.

3. Put rum ingredients into a large (1 gallon/3.8 liter) zip-closure cooking pouch, evacuate the air (page 11), and seal.

4. Put ginger syrup ingredients into a large (1 gallon/3.8 liter) zip-closure cooking pouch, evacuate the air (page 11), and seal.

5. Submerge the pouches in the water oven. Cook the ginger syrup for 2 hours and the red pepper rum for 3 hours.

6. Remove the pouches and submerge them in an ice water bath (half ice, half water) for 20 to 30 minutes to quick-chill the contents.

7. Strain the mixtures through a fine mesh sieve into clean bottles, and discard the solids.

8. Store, tightly-capped, labeled and dated, in the refrigerator for up to six weeks. Optional: adding 2 ounces (60 ml) of vodka per quart (0.9 liter) of finished ginger syrup will add a couple of weeks to the shelf life.

red rum daisy

Makes 1 cocktail

1. In a cocktail shaker, mix all ingredients, except ice and garnish.

2. Mound ice in a cocktail or coupe glass and pour the contents from the shaker over the ice.

3. Top with more crushed ice and a lime twist.

For the red pepper rum

2 whole red bell peppers

1 bottle (25 oz/750 ml) Appleton gold rum

For the ginger syrup

4 cups (32 oz/946 ml) ginger juice *

2 cups (13 oz/385 g) superfine (castor) sugar

1 cup (8 oz/240 ml) water

red rum daisy

$1^1/_2$ ounces (45 ml) red pepper rum

1 ounce (30 ml) ginger syrup

$^3/_4$ ounce (22.5 ml) lime juice

$^1/_2$ ounce (15 ml) grenadine

$^1/_2$ cup (4 oz/240 ml) shaved or crushed ice

Lime twist, for garnish

* Juice whole fresh ginger root (about 2 pounds) or ask your local juice bar to juice it for you.

raspberry syrup

1 pint (300 g) raspberries

2 cups (13 oz/385 g) superfine (castor) sugar

2 cups (8 oz/480 ml) water

Clover Club cocktail

1 ounce (30 ml) lemon juice

$^1/_2$ ounce (15 ml) raspberry syrup

1 egg white

$1^1/_2$ ounces (45 ml) gin

Ice cubes

Courtesy of Chef Brian McCracken and Chef Dana Tough

Makes 450 ml
Cooking time: 2 hours

1. Fill and preheat the water oven to 135°F (57°C).

2. Put the raspberries, sugar and water into a large (1 gallon/3.8 liter) zip-closure cooking pouch, evacuate the air (page 11), and seal.

3. Submerge the pouch in the water oven and cook for 2 hours.

4. Remove the pouch and submerge it in an ice water bath (half ice, half water) for 20 to 30 minutes to quick-chill the contents.

5. Strain the syrup through a fine mesh sieve into a clean bottle and discard the berries or save to use for another purpose.

6. Store, tightly-capped, labeled and dated, in the refrigerator for up to 6 weeks. Optional: adding 2 ounces (60 ml) of vodka per quart (0.9 liter) of finished liquid will add a couple of weeks to the shelf life.

Clover Club cocktail

Makes 1 cocktail

1. Put all ingredients, except gin and ice, into a cocktail shaker.

2. Shake vigorously until the egg white is frothy.

3. Add ice cubes and gin and shake again.

4. Strain into a large coupe or flip glass.*

* A coupe glass is a shallow, broad-bowled, stemmed glass customarily used for champagne. A flip glass is a drinking tumbler originating from the 17th and 18th Centuries, often cylindrical or with gently flaring sides.

falernum

4 cups (32 oz/946 ml) simple syrup

1 cup (8 oz/237 ml) light rum

5 limes for zest only

4 drops almond extract

8 whole cloves

5 whole allspice berries

2 drops orange flower water

new frisco cocktail

1 cup (8 oz/240 ml) crushed ice

$1^{1}/_{2}$ ounces (45 ml) Calvados

$^{1}/_{2}$ ounce (15 ml) lemon juice

$^{1}/_{2}$ ounce (15 ml) falernum

$^{1}/_{2}$ ounce (15 ml) Benedictine

1 dash Angostura bitters

Courtesy of Chef Brian McCracken and Chef Dana Tough

Makes 1.2 liters
Cooking time: 2 hours

1. Fill and preheat the water oven to 135°F (57°C).

2. Put all ingredients into a large (1 gallon/3.8 liter) zip-closure cooking pouch, evacuate the air (page 11), and seal.

3. Submerge the pouch in the water oven and cook for 2 hours.

4. Remove the pouch and submerge it in an ice water bath (half ice, half water) for 20 to 30 minutes to quick-chill the contents.

5. Strain the mixture through a fine mesh sieve into a clean bottle.

6. Store the falernum, tightly-capped, in the refrigerator for up to six weeks.

new frisco cocktail

Courtesy of Nathan Weber

Makes 1 cocktail

1. Put crushed ice into a rocks or bucket glass.

2. Build the cocktail in the glass, adding one ingredient at a time in the order listed.

3. Stir gently and serve.

rum shrub

1 cup (8 oz/240 ml) Appleton gold rum

1 cup (8 oz/240 ml) falernum (recipe on page 29)

1 cup (8 oz/240 ml) lemon juice

1 cup (8 oz/240 ml) orange juice

4 oranges for zest

Courtesy of Chef Brian McCracken and Chef Dana Tough

Makes 960 ml
Cooking time: 2 hours

1. Fill and preheat the water oven to 125°F (51.5°C).

2. With a vegetable peeler, remove the zest from the oranges in wide ribbons, taking care to avoid getting the white pith, which is bitter.

3. Put the orange zest and all remaining ingredients into a zip-closure cooking pouch, evacuate the air (page 11), and seal.

3. Submerge the pouch in the water oven and cook for 2 hours.

4. Remove the pouch from the water bath and submerge it in an ice water bath (half ice, half water) for 20 to 30 minutes to quick-chill the contents.

5. Strain the mixture through a fine mesh sieve into a clean bottle and discard the solids.

6. Store, tightly-capped, labeled and dated, in the refrigerator for up to six weeks.

sunrise cocktail

sunrise cocktail

2 ounces (60 ml) rum shrub

$^1/_2$ ounce (15 ml) Cointreau

$^1/_4$ ounce (7.5 ml) raspberry syrup (recipe on page 27)

2 dashes Angostura bitters

3 to 4 ounces (90 to 120 ml) champagne

Lemon twist, for garnish

Courtesy of Nathan Weber

Makes 1 cocktail

1. Pour all ingredients except for the champagne and garnish into a mixing glass.

2. Add ice and stir.

3. Strain into a champagne flute and top with champagne.

4. Garnish with a lemon twist.

peach brandy

4 ripe peaches
1 bottle (25 oz/750 ml) brandy

fish house punch
Ice cubes
1 ounce (30 ml) peach brandy
1 ounce (30 ml) gold rum
1 ounce (30 ml) lemon juice
$3/4$ ounce (22.5 ml) simple syrup
Cherries, lemon slices, or peach slices for garnish

Courtesy of Chef Brian McCracken and Chef Dana Tough

Makcs 750 ml
Cooking time: 1 hour

1. Fill and preheat the water oven to 177°F (80.5°C).

2. Cut all peaches in half; remove and discard the pit from three of them, but leave it in the fourth.

3. Put the ingredients into a large (1 gallon/3.8 liter) zip-closure cooking pouch, evacuate the air (page 11), and seal.

4. Submerge the pouch in the water oven and cook for 1 hour.

5. Remove the pouch and submerge it in an ice water bath (half ice, half water) for 30 minutes to quick-chill the contents.

6. Strain the brandy through a fine mesh sieve into a clean bottle.

7. Store, tightly-capped, labeled and dated, in the refrigerator for up to six weeks.

fish house punch

1. Fill a cocktail shaker about half full with ice cubes.

2. Build the cocktail in the shaker, adding all ingredients, and shake.

3. Pour the cocktail into a rocks or bucket glass and garnish with fresh fruit of your choice.

pineapple syrup

Courtesy of Chef Brian McCracken and Chef Dana Tough

Makes 473 ml
Cooking time: 2 hours

1. Fill and preheat the water oven to 135°F (57°C).

2. Put pineapple, sugar and water into a large (1 gallon/3.8 liter) zip-closure cooking pouch, evacuate the air (page 11), and seal.

3. Submerge the pouch in the water oven and cook for 2 hours.

4. Remove the pouch and submerge it in an ice water bath (half ice, half water) for 20 to 30 minutes to quick-chill the contents.

5. Open the pouch, add the gum Arabic and whisk to blend well.

6. Strain the syrup through a fine mesh sieve into a clean bottle.

7. Store, tightly-capped, labeled and dated, in the refrigerator for up to six weeks. Optional: adding 2 ounces (60 ml) of vodka per quart (0.9 liter) of finished liquid will add a couple of weeks to the shelf life.

Pisco punch

Courtesy of Nathan Weber

Makes 1 cocktail

1. Add all ingredients, in the order given, to a cocktail shaker and shake well.

2. Pour over ice in a rocks or bucket glass.

3. Garnish with a pineapple slice, if desired.

$1/2$ fresh pineapple, trimmed and peeled

2 cups (13 oz/385 g) superfine (castor) sugar

2 cups (16 oz/473 ml) water

5 ounces (148 g) gum Arabic*

Pisco punch

$1\frac{1}{2}$ ounces (45 ml) Pisco**

1 ounce (30 ml) Pineapple Syrup

1 ounce (30 ml) fresh Key lime juice

1 dash of Angostura bitters

1 dash of Absinthe (optional)

4 small slices fresh pineapple (optional for garnish)

* Gum Arabic is a natural stabilizer made from the sap of the acacia tree, and used extensively in food manufacture. It is readily available online and in specialty stores.

** Pisco is a pale gold or colorless Peruvian or Chilean grape brandy.

starters

35

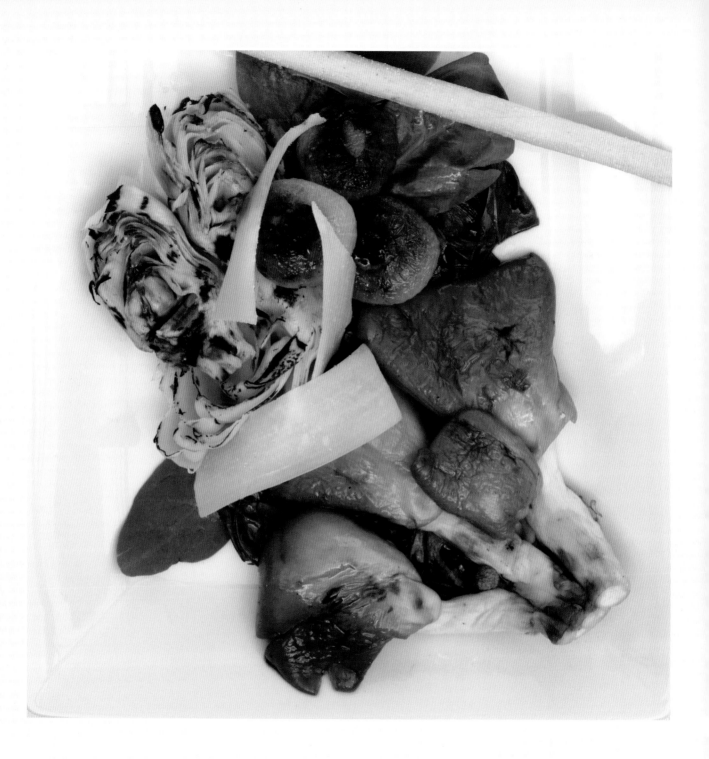

artichoke salad with grissini bread sticks

Courtesy of Chef Alex Seidel

Serves 4
Cooking time: 2 hours

Cook the artichokes

1. Fill and preheat the water oven to 185°F (85°C).

2. Fill a bowl, large enough to hold the artichokes, with water and add the juice of the two lemons.

3. Clean the artichokes using a vegetable peeler and cut them in half. Immediately drop the halves into the acidulated (lemon) water to keep them from oxidizing.

4. Remove the artichokes from the water and put them in a single, even layer into a large (1 gallon/3.8 liter) zip-closure cooking pouch. Add the vegetable stock, a drizzle of olive oil and sprinkle of salt, evacuate the air from the pouch (page 11) and seal.

5. Submerge the pouch in the water oven and cook for 90 minutes.

6. Quick chill, submerged in an ice water bath (half ice, half water) for 15 to 20 minutes. Open the pouch, remove 12 halves to reserve for plating. The remainder will be used for the artichoke dip.

Make the grissini bread sticks

1. Preheat the traditional oven to 350°F (176.5°C).

2. In a small mixing bowl combine the yeast, water, and sugar and proof for 4 or 5 minutes (bubbles will begin to form as the yeast begins to work.)

3. After the yeast mixture has proofed, add it to the bowl of an electric mixer, add the milk, and mix on low speed to incorporate.

4. Add the flour and olive oil and knead at low speed until it makes a well-formed ball that pulls away from the sides of the bowl.

5. Cover the bowl and move it to a warm place in the kitchen to let the dough rise.

6. When the dough has doubled in size, punch down.

For the salad

1 quart (32 oz/0.9 liters) water

2 lemons

36 fresh baby artichokes, divided use

2 cups (16 oz/473 ml) vegetable stock

2 tablespoons (15 ml) olive oil

Salt, to taste

For the grissini bread sticks

$1/2$ tablespoon (7.5 ml) dry active yeast

$1/4$ cup (2 oz/60 ml) water at body temperature: 98°F (37°C)

$1^1/2$ tablespoons (22.5 ml) sugar

$1/2$ cup (4 oz/120 ml) milk

2 cups (9.6 oz/272 g) bread flour

$1^1/2$ tablespoons (22.5 ml) olive oil

For the artichoke dip

2 cups (16 oz/473 ml) heavy cream

$1/2$ cup (3 oz/90 g) grated Parmigiano-Reggiano (or other Parmesan cheese)

Salt and white pepper to taste

3 cups (3.2 oz/90 g) spinach, blanched and drained well

$1/2$ cup (4 oz/113 g) cream cheese

2 tablespoons (30 ml) fresh oregano leaves

For plating

12 cipollini onions

4 cups (4.2 oz/120 g) fresh spinach

12 reserved baby artichoke halves

1 cup (2.5 oz/70 g) oyster mushrooms

Aged balsamic vinegar, for garnish

Parmigiano-Reggiano, shaved, for garnish

artichoke salad with grissini bread sticks

continued from page 37

7. Roll the dough flat, using either a pasta roller or a rolling pin, to a ¼-inch (0.6 cm) thickness.

8. Cut the dough into strips ¼-inch (0.6 cm) wide and 6-inches (9.5 cm) long.

9. Roll each strip by hand to form into a round stick.

10. Put the sticks on a parchment-lined baking sheet and bake until crispy and slightly golden brown—about 15 minutes.

Make the artichoke dip

1. In a heavy saucepan, reduce the cream by half.

2. Add 30 of the baby artichoke halves and Parmesan and season with salt and white pepper.

3. Rough chop 30 more of the artichoke halves and reserve.

4. Rough chop half the spinach and reserve.

5. In a food service blender or food processor, put the artichoke cream mixture, remaining spinach, cream cheese and oregano, and blend until smooth.

6. Push the mixture through a fine mesh strainer and cool.

7. When the mixture has cooled, fold in the reserved chopped artichokes and spinach.

Finish the salad and plate

1. Caramelize the cipollini onions in a large sauté pan over medium heat with a bit of olive oil until they are golden all over. Set aside.

2. Grill the fresh spinach and the 12 reserved artichoke halves on an oiled grill or grill pan to warm and mark them.

3. In a skillet, sauté the oyster mushrooms.

4. Warm the artichoke dip on the stove top.

5. On one end of a rectangular plate, mound artichoke dip in a ring mold, press gently and remove ring.

6. Pile grilled spinach down the length of the plate.

7. Arrange the mushrooms, onions, and grilled artichokes on top of the spinach.

8. Garnish with drops of aged balsamic and curls of shaved Parmigianino-Reggiano.

9. Place 2 or 3 bread sticks diagonally across the plate.

chicken galantine

Courtesy of Pam McKinstry

Serves 6 to 8
Cooking time: 1½ to 2 hours

Prepare the stuffing

1. Put the chicken, egg, shallot, tarragon, garlic, salt, and pepper in a food processor and pulse to combine.

2. Add cream and Marsala and process until the mixture is smooth, about 2 minutes, stopping to scrape down the sides of the bowl once or twice.

3. Transfer the mixture to a bowl or container, stir in the nuts, cover, and refrigerate until completely chilled, at least 4 hours or overnight.

Assemble the galantine

1. Lay an 18 x 24-inch (46 x 60 cm) piece of microwavable plastic wrap (cling film) on clean work surface—a large cutting board is perfect —with the long edge at the top.

2. Center one slice of prosciutto 5 inches (13 cm) below the top edge.

3. Arrange a second slice, slightly overlapping the first piece of prosciutto. Continue in this manner until you have used all but 2 slices of the prosciutto. You should have a rectangle of prosciutto that measures roughly 6 inches (15 cm) tall by 11 inches (28 cm) long.

4. Transfer the chicken mixture to the center of the prosciutto rectangle and form it (lengthwise) into a log of even thickness. Use your hands to do this.

5. Place the remaining 2 pieces of prosciutto lengthwise on top of the log (this will ensure that the filling is enclosed if the prosciutto rectangle does not completely cover the chicken mixture).

6. Pick up the long edge of plastic wrap (cling film) nearest you and use it to roll the prosciutto over the filling. Continue rolling gently, pulling back the plastic as you roll, until the chicken log is completely encased in the prosciutto. Then wrap the entire log in the plastic wrap.

7. Twist the ends of the plastic wrap to make a tight sausage, using your hands to keep the roll an even thickness. Tie a knot in each end as close to the mixture as possible. The galantine should measure approximately 10 inches (25 cm) in length by 2 inches (5 cm) in diameter.

For the stuffing

1 pound (16 oz/473 g) ground chicken

1 large egg

¼ cup (1.4 oz/40 g) minced shallot

2 tablespoons (30 ml) chopped fresh tarragon

2 large cloves garlic, peeled and crushed

2 teaspoons (10 ml) kosher salt

1 teaspoon (5 ml) freshly ground black pepper

⅔ cup (5.3 oz/157 ml) heavy (whipping) cream

2 tablespoons (30 ml) Marsala

⅓ cup (1.6 oz/48 g) roughly chopped hazelnuts

For the galantine

6 ounces (177 g) very thinly sliced prosciutto

2 tablespoons (30 ml) olive oil

chicken galantine

continued from page 39

8. Chill the galantine in the refrigerator for at least 1 hour.

Cook the chicken galantine

1. Fill and preheat the water oven to 158°F (70°C).

2. When the water is at temperature, remove the galantine from the refrigerator and put it into a large (1 gallon/3.8 liter) cooking pouch and vacuum seal.

3. Submerge the pouch in the water oven and cook for 1½ to 2 hours.

4. Remove the galantine from the pouch and transfer to a clean work surface. Remove the plastic wrap (cling film).

5. Heat a large skillet, preferably cast-iron, over medium-high heat. Using paper towels, dry the surface of the galantine.

6. When the skillet is hot, add the olive oil and sear the galantine on all sides until the prosciutto is golden and crisp.

7. To serve hot, slice and serve immediately.

8. If not serving immediately, transfer the galantine to a platter and let it cool to room temperature. Tightly wrap the galantine in clean plastic wrap (cling film) and refrigerate until it is chilled. The galantine will keep under refrigeration for up to 5 days.

9. To serve cold, unwrap the galantine and cut it into ⅓- to ½-inch (0.8- to 1.3-cm) thick slices. Serve with a salad of arugula or watercress.

Asian tuna salad

Courtesy of Michael Vetsch

Serves 2
Cooking time: 1 hour

1. Fill and preheat the water oven to 125°F (51.5°C).

2. In a bowl combine the sesame oil, rice vinegar, olive oil, half the cilantro, the garlic, and the chiles.

3. Gently toss the tuna in the combined mixture, add all to a cooking pouch and vacuum seal.

4. Submerge the pouch in the water oven and cook for 45 minutes to 1 hour.

5. Remove the tuna from the pouch and allow it to cool.

6. In a bowl combine the Sweet Thai Chili Sauce, the rest of the cilantro and the lime juice.

7. Flake the tuna or serve whole on a bed of mixed greens and drizzle with the dressing. Garnish as desired.

2 ahi or albacore tuna filets about 5 to 6 ounces (142 to 170 g) each

Salt and pepper, to taste

1 teaspoon (5 ml) sesame oil

2 teaspoons (10 ml) rice vinegar

2 tablespoons (30 ml) extra virgin olive oil

1 bunch cilantro, chopped

1 clove garlic, chopped

2 serrano chiles, chopped

1 small bottle Sweet Thai Chili Sauce

Juice of 1 lime

Mixed greens

fresh beet salad

Adapted from *The Low Carb Comfort Food Cookbook*,
Eades and Solom (Wiley, 2005)

Serves 4
Cooking time: 1 hour

1. Fill and preheat the water oven to 182–185°F (83–85°C).

2. Vacuum seal the beets in a large (1 gallon/3.8 liter) cooking pouch.

3. Cook for at least 1 hour (up to 2 hours.)

4. At this point, either quick chill the beets in their pouch in ice water (half ice, half water) and refrigerate for up to 48 hours, or allow the beets to cool slightly and proceed.

5. Peel the beets, dice them into $\frac{1}{2}$-inch pieces, and put them in a bowl.

6. Peel the mandarins, separate them into segments, and combine them with the beets.

7. In a small bowl, make a light vinaigrette by combining the vinegar, salt, and chives and allowing the mixture to sit for a few minutes.

8. Whisk the olive oil into the vinegar and pour over the beet and orange mixture, tossing to coat.

9. Chill for at least 10 minutes (or up to several hours).

10. When ready to serve, divide the fresh greens among four chilled plates, top with one-quarter of the beets and oranges, sprinkle with feta, and serve.

For the salad

1 pound (16 oz/454 g) fresh beets, trimmed, well scrubbed, and cut in half

4 cups (10.5 oz/300 grams) freshly torn salad greens

$\frac{1}{2}$ cup (70 g) mandarin supreme oranges (canned or fresh)

For the vinaigrette

2 tablespoons (30 ml) sherry vinegar

$\frac{1}{2}$ teaspoon (2.5 ml) salt

1 tablespoon (15 ml) fresh chives, minced

1 tablespoon (15 ml) extra virgin olive oil

For garnish

$\frac{1}{2}$ cup (75 g) crumbled feta

Asian shrimp

Courtesy of Chef Josh Horrigan

Serves 4 to 6
Cooking time: 25 minutes

Make the cocktail sauce

1. Combine all cocktail sauce ingredients in a bowl and mix well.

2. Chill for 4 to 5 hours.

Make the marinade

1. Toast the peppercorns, cumin and coriander seeds and grind them together.

2. In a cooking pouch, combine the olive oil with all the other ingredients except the shrimp and set into the freezer to become solid. (It doesn't have to be frozen rock hard, just thick enough to prevent the vacuum from sucking it into the sealing chamber when vacuum sealing the shrimp.)

Cook the shrimp

1. Fill and preheat the water oven to 122°F (50°C).

2. Put the shrimp in a single layer into the cooking pouch with the frozen seasoned oil, and vacuum seal.

3. Submerge the pouch in the water bath to cook for 25 minutes.

4. Remove the shrimp from the pouch and pat dry.

5. Put the shrimp onto a parchment-paper-lined baking sheet and chill completely for about an hour.

6. To serve, line a martini glass with a bed of shredded Napa cabbage. Add the chilled shrimp, drizzle generously with cocktail sauce, and garnish with a lime.

For the cocktail sauce

1 cup (240 ml) ketchup

$1/2$ cup (120 ml) Mae Ploy sweet Thai chili sauce

1 tablespoon (15 ml) Sriracha hot sauce

2 limes, for juice

2 tablespoons (30 ml) soy sauce, or to taste

$1^1/2$ teaspoon (7.5 ml) minced ginger root

1 serrano pepper (keep veins and seeds for more heat if you like)

1 tablespoon (12 g) brown sugar

$1/2$ cup (20 g) finely chopped cilantro leaves

$1/8$ cup (20 g) finely minced radishes

$1/2$ teaspoon (2.5 ml) cumin powder

$1/2$ teaspoon (2.5 ml) coriander powder

2 tablespoons (30 ml) wasabi powder

For the shrimp marinade

$1/2$ teaspoon (2.5 ml) Sichuan peppercorns, toasted

$1/2$ teaspoon (2.5 ml) cumin seeds, toasted

$1/2$ teaspoon (2.5 ml) coriander seeds, toasted

$1/2$ cup (120 ml) extra virgin olive oil

$1/2$ teaspoon (2.5 ml) sea salt

1 tablespoon (15 ml) mild red chili powder

18 U-10 raw shrimp, peeled and deveined, tails on

For plating

Napa cabbage

1 lime, sliced

confit of salmon

Courtesy of Chef Raymond Blanc

Serves 4
Cooking time: 4 to 8 hours

Prepare the cucumbers

1. The night before, cut the cucumber into ribbons, salt them, and marinate for 25 minutes. Wash off the salt, pat dry, and freeze overnight.

2. Defrost cucumber ribbons at room temperature, taste, and wash off any excess salt.

Cook the salmon

1. Fill and preheat the water oven to 107°F (42°C).

2. Season the salmon pieces with the salt, sugar and pepper, sprinkle with chopped dill and lemon zest.

3. Put the seasoned salmon pieces into a cooking pouch and vacuum seal.

4. Submerge the pouch in the water oven to cook for 20 minutes.

Prepare the vegetables

1. Make the mustard dressing by whisking together the vinegar and mustard; drizzle in the oil until combined and add the dill. Taste and correct the seasoning.

2. Toss the cucumber ribbons with the dressing to lightly coat.

3. In a bowl, mix the cauliflower florets with the remaining ingredients, taste, and reserve for the plate.

Plate and serve

1. Remove the salmon pieces from the pouch and place each piece in the middle of a serving plate.

2. Scatter the cucumber ribbons and cauliflower florets around the salmon, garnish with a few micro herbs and serve.

For the cucumber salad

3 pinches (3 g) sea salt

$^1/_2$ cucumber, peeled, deseeded and cut into 4-inch x $^1/_8$-inch (12-cm x 2-mm) ribbons

For the salmon

5 ounces (140g) organic farmed salmon, filleted, boned, skinned, and cut into 4 pieces

2 pinches (2 g) sea salt

1 pinch (1 g) castor sugar

1 pinch (1 g) white pepper

1 teaspoon (5 g) chopped dill

$^1/_4$ lemon, for zest only

For the mustard dressing

2 teaspoons (10 ml) white wine vinegar

1 tablespoon (15 ml) Dijon mustard

2 tablespoons (30ml) grapeseed oil

1 tablespoon (15 ml) chopped dill

For the cauliflower

1 cup (80g) cauliflower florets

1 teaspoon (5ml) horseradish sauce

2 tablespoons (30 ml) crème fraîche

1 pinch (1 g) sea salt

1 pinch (1 g) cayenne pepper

$^1/_2$ teaspoon (2.5 ml) lemon juice

For plating

Microgreens

Thai lettuce wraps

Serves 4
Cooking time: 1½ to 4 hours

1. Fill and preheat the water oven to 146°F (63°C).

2. In a small bowl, mix the coconut oil with the salt, pepper, curry paste, and ginger.

3. Divide the coconut oil mixture between two small (1 quart/0.9 liter) cooking pouches.

4. Put two chicken breast halves into each pouch in a single layer and vacuum seal.

5. Submerge the pouches in the water oven and cook for 90 minutes and up to 4 hours.

Make the peanut sauce

1. In a small bowl, combine the peanut butter, soy sauce and vinegar, and mix well.

2. Add hot sauce to taste, and set aside.

Finish the chicken

1. Remove the breasts from the pouches and let cool enough to handle, then dice.

2. To serve, arrange the lettuce leaves, julienne vegetables, and chicken on a platter. Top with the cilantro. Serve the peanut sauce on the side.

1 tablespoon (15 ml) coconut oil

1 teaspoon (5 ml) salt

1 teaspoon (5 ml) black pepper

1 teaspoon (5 ml) Thai red curry paste

½ teaspoon (2.5 ml) ground ginger

4 boneless, skinless chicken breast halves

8 to 10 butter lettuce leaves, washed and trimmed

1 carrot, peeled and cut into thin 1-inch (2.5 cm) julienne strips

1 cucumber, peeled, seeded and cut into 1-inch (2.5 cm) julienne strips

For the peanut sauce

2 tablespoons (30 ml) peanut butter

2 tablespoons (30 ml) lite soy sauce

1 tablespoon (15 ml) rice wine vinegar

1 dash Tabasco® hot sauce (or more to taste)

1 bunch fresh cilantro, for garnish

entrées

beef

tri-tip sirloin with cilantro butter 53

Thai beef tenderloin 54

Korean barbecue short ribs 55

rainy day rib-eye steaks 57

blackberry pear filet mignon 58

corned beef and cabbage 59

Yemenite spiced ribs with celery salad 61

beef rib roast 62

Asian short ribs 63

Balti beef 65

 sous vide beef tenderloin video
scan the code with your smart phone,
or visit sousvidesupreme.com/thecookbook

sous vide steak video
scan the code with your smart phone,
or visit sousvidesupreme.com/thecookbook

tri-tip sirloin with cilantro butter

Serves 4
Cooking time: 3 to 12 hours

1. Fill and preheat the water oven to 134°F (56.5°C).

2. Season the sirloin with salt and pepper.

3. Transfer to a large (1 gallon/3.8 liter) cooking pouch and vacuum seal.

4. Submerge the pouch in the water oven and cook for at least 3 hours, and up to 12 hours for fork-tender results.

5. In a bowl, mix the shallots with the lime juice; let stand for 10 minutes.

6. Meanwhile, using a handheld mixer, beat the butter, chipotle and cilantro at low speed until blended. Set aside.

7. Brush a skillet or grill grate with oil and preheat on high heat.

8. Remove the meat from the pouch, and pat it dry.

9. Sear the steak until browned and crusty, 30 seconds per side.

10. Thinly slice the steak and serve with the cilantro butter.

1 pound (16 oz/0.45 kg) tri-tip sirloin, about 2 inches (5 cm) thick

1 teaspoon (5 ml) kosher salt

1 teaspoon (5 ml) cracked pepper

2 teaspoons (10 ml) minced shallot

2 teaspoons (10 ml) lime juice

Vegetable oil for searing

For the cilantro butter

1 stick salted butter, softened

2 chipotle chiles in adobo, stemmed, seeded and minced

3 tablespoons (45 ml) chopped cilantro leaves

53

Thai beef tenderloin

4 (8-ounce/227-g) filets of beef tenderloin, about $1\frac{1}{2}$ inches (4 cm) thick

$\frac{1}{3}$ cup (75 ml) peanut oil

4 cloves garlic, peeled and sliced

2 shallots, peeled and thinly sliced

2 tablespoons (30 ml) chopped rosemary

2 tablespoons (30 ml) chopped thyme

1 lime, zest only

1 orange, zest only

2 tablespoons (30 ml) Asian fish sauce

$\frac{1}{3}$ cup (75 ml) low-sodium soy sauce

10 dried Thai chiles, coarsely chopped

1 tablespoon (15 ml) unsalted butter

1 tablespoon (15 ml) extra-virgin olive oil

Serves 4
Cooking time: 1 to 3 hours

1. Fill and preheat the water oven to 134°F (56.5°C).

2. In a small saucepan, heat the vegetable oil and sauté the garlic over low heat until soft, about 3 minutes.

3. Remove the garlic pieces from the oil and drain them on paper towels. Reserve the oil; let it cool to room temperature.

4. Using a sharp paring knife, make $\frac{1}{2}$-inch (1.3 cm) slits all over the tenderloin steaks and stuff the slits with the sautéed garlic pieces.

5. Fill a large (1 gallon/3.8 liter) zip-closure bag with the shallots, rosemary, thyme, lime zest, orange zest, fish sauce, soy sauce, dried chiles and the reserved garlic oil. Add the steaks and seal, turning to coat the meat with the marinade. Let stand at room temperature for 2 hours.

6. Pour off marinade into a small saucepan and reserve for later use.

7. Vacuum seal the filets, 1 or 2 to a small (1 quart/0.9 liter) zip-closure cooking pouch. Evacuate the air from the pouch (page 11) and seal.

8. Submerge the pouches in the water oven, being sure the meat is entirely below the surface of the water for even cooking.

9. Cook for at least 1 hour, and up to 3 hours.

10. Meanwhile, in a small saucepan, bring the reserved marinade to a boil, reduce heat, and simmer to keep warm as a sauce to serve with the steaks.

11. In a skillet large enough to hold the filets comfortably (or working in batches to avoid overcrowding the pan) melt the butter in the olive oil and heat until nearly smoking.

12. Remove the steaks from the pouches and pat dry.

14. Sear the filets in the skillet 15-20 seconds per side, turning once, to form a brown crust.

15. Serve immediately, topped with sauce.

Korean barbecue short ribs

Serves 6
Cooking time: 48 hours

Make the marinade

1. In a medium bowl, whisk together the soy sauce, garlic, ginger, scallions, sugar, and sesame oil.

2. Season with black pepper.

3. Use the marinade immediately or refrigerate in a tightly sealed container for up to 2 days.

Marinate the short ribs

1. Place the ribs in a single layer in a large glass baking dish. Pour about three-quarters of the marinade over the ribs, and turn them to coat evenly. Reserve the remaining marinade for serving.

2. Cover the dish and refrigerate; allow the ribs to marinate for at least 2 hours or up to 8 hours.

Cook the short ribs

1. Fill and preheat the water oven to 132°F (55.5°C).

2. Remove the ribs from the marinade and blot them with a damp paper towel.

3. Put the ribs into cooking pouches in a single layer (4 rib squares per 1 quart/0.9 liter pouch) and vacuum seal.

4. Submerge the pouches in the water bath and cook for 48 hours.

5. Oil the grate of a gas or charcoal grill and preheat to high heat.

6. Remove the ribs from the cooking pouches, pat them dry, and sear them on the grill, meaty side down until browned, approximately 1 minute per side. (Alternately, sear in a very hot sauté pan with a little bit of peanut oil until browned, approximately 1 minute per side.)

7. Serve with a side of reserved marinade for dipping.

6 pounds (2.72 kg) beef short ribs, cut crosswise into twelve 2½-inch (6.4 cm) squares (ask your butcher to cut the ribs for you)

Peanut oil

For the marinade

1 cup (240 ml) soy sauce*

4 large cloves garlic, peeled and chopped or (already prepared minced)

2 tablespoons (30 ml) finely grated peeled fresh ginger or (already prepared minced)

4 scallions, thinly sliced

¼ cup (1.8 oz/50 g) sugar

2 tablespoons (30 ml) sesame oil

Freshly ground black pepper

* Not all soy sauces are the same. Some are saltier, others sweet and thick. For the best results with this marinade, choose a dark Japanese or Korean soy sauce.

rainy day
ribeye steaks

Courtesy of Sally MacColl

Serves 2
Cooking time: 1½ to 3 hours

1. Fill and preheat the water oven to 134°F (56.5°C).

2. Trim the steaks of excess outside fat; rinse them and pat dry.

3. In a small bowl, combine all seasonings except the vegetable oil and butter, and mix well.

4. Rub one side of the steaks with half the oil and sprinkle half the seasoning mixture over them. Flip steaks over and repeat.

5. Put each steak into a small (1 quart/0.9 liter) cooking pouch and vacuum seal. (At this point, the steaks can be refrigerated for up to a day in advance of cooking.)

6. Submerge the pouches in the water oven and cook the steaks for a minimum of 90 minutes or up to 3 hours. (Substantially longer cooking times can result in a too-soft texture.)

7. Remove the steaks from the pouches and drain the accumulated juices into a small bowl or ramekin; set aside.

8. Lightly pat the steaks with paper towels to dry the surface.

9. Heat a skillet large enough to hold both steaks over medium-high heat until the pan is very hot. If using butter, add 2 tablespoons (30 ml) to the hot pan and immediately add the steaks. Sear the meat for 1 minute, then turn and sear the other side for 30 seconds. Immediately transfer the steaks to warm serving plates.

10. For the optional pan sauce, add the reserved cooking juices to the skillet and cook until reduced by half, about 1 minute.

11. Remove the pan from the heat and whisk in the remaining 1 tablespoon (15 ml) of butter.

12. Pour the sauce over the steaks and serve immediately.

2 boneless ribeye steaks, 1 to 1½ inches (2.5 cm to 3.8 cm) thick

2 cloves garlic, finely minced or pressed

2 teaspoons (10 ml) finely grated lemon zest

1 teaspoon (5 ml) truffle salt or more to taste

1 teaspoon (5 ml) ground fennel seed

1 teaspoon (5 ml) smoked paprika

1 teaspoon (5 ml) freshly ground black pepper

2 tablespoons (30 ml) vegetable oil

3 tablespoons (45 ml) butter, divided use (optional)

blackberry pear filet mignon

Courtesy of Stephanie Stiavetti

Serves 2
Cooking time: 1 to 4 hours

2 filet mignon steaks, about 2 inches (5 cm) thick

1 fresh pear, whatever type is in season

$^1/_2$ cup (4 oz/120 ml) high-quality balsamic vinegar

2 tablespoons (30 ml) blackberry jam

1 tablespoon (15 ml) flaky sea salt

1 teaspoon (15 ml) freshly ground black pepper

2 tablespoons (60 ml) butter

1. Fill and preheat the water oven to 134°F (56.5°C) for medium-rare; 140°F (60°C) for medium; or 150°F (65.5°C) for medium-well.

2. Pat steaks dry and set aside.

3. Peel the pear, then cut it in half, remove the seeds, and purée in a food processor until smooth.

4. In a small saucepan over a medium heat, combine the balsamic vinegar, blackberry jam and 2 tablespoons of the pear purée. Stirring occasionally, heat the mixture until it has thickened substantially, about 15 minutes.

5. Once the sauce has adequately reduced, remove it from the heat.

6. Give the steaks a final pat down to remove any remaining moisture. Sprinkle both sides with salt and pepper, and drop a tablespoon-full of the reduction onto each steak, giving it a little swirl to cover the surface. Reserve the remainder of the reduction sauce.

7. Put both steaks into a small (1 quart/0.9 liter) cooking pouch and vacuum seal.

8. Put the pouch into the water bath, making sure the meat is fully submerged to ensure even cooking.

9. Cook for 1 hour, and no longer than 4 hours. (Longer cooking times can result in a too-soft texture.)

10. When steaks have just about finished cooking, reheat the reserved blackberry pear reduction sauce over a medium-low flame. Swirl in the butter and leave the sauce simmering over a very low heat once the butter is melted. Occasionally stir with a spatula or wooden spoon to keep from burning.

11. Meanwhile, heat a small skillet over medium-high heat for a minute or two.

12. Remove the steaks from the cooking pouch, pat them dry, and sear each side for 30 seconds or so in the hot skillet.

13. Serve immediately, topped with the blackberry pear sauce.

corned beef and cabbage

Serves 6 to 8
Cooking time: 48 hours

4 pounds (1.81 kg) corned beef

6 slices of bacon, cut into ½-inch (1.3 cm) strips

1 head of cabbage, cut into 1-inch (3 cm) strips

2 cups (10 oz/473 ml) chicken stock

½ cup (4 oz/120 ml) champagne vinegar

1. Fill and preheat the water oven to 134°F (56.5°C).

2. Put the corned beef into a cooking pouch and vacuum seal.

3. Submerge the pouch in the water oven and cook for 48 hours

4. About 45 minutes before you are ready to serve the meal, prepare the cabbage.

5. In a skillet, over medium heat, cook the bacon pieces until they are crisp and the fat is rendered. Pour off all but 1-2 tablespoons (15 to 30 ml) of the bacon fat.

6. Add the cabbage strips to the skillet, raise the heat to medium-high, and cook for about 5 minutes.

7. Add the chicken stock and the vinegar to the pan and continue to cook the cabbage in the liquid until tender.

8. When the cabbage is almost tender, remove the corned beef from the water bath and the cooking pouch.

9. To serve, slice the corned beef into ½- to ¾-inch (1.3 to 2 cm) slices and serve atop the cabbage.

Yemenite spiced ribs with celery salad

Courtesy of Chef Michael Solomonov, Zahav, Philadelphia

Serves 4
Cooking time: 24½ to hours

1. Fill and preheat the water oven to 145°F (63°C).

2. In a small bowl, mix together the spices and the salt and distribute evenly over the short ribs.

3. Put the ribs, two to a pouch in a single layer, into small (1 quart/0.9 liter) cooking pouches, and vacuum seal.

4. Submerge the pouches in the water bath and cook for 24 hours.

A few minutes before the ribs are done, make the celery salad

1. Coarsely chop the celery, dates, and parsley.

2. Add the lemon juice, and mix well.

3. Season with kosher salt to taste.

Finish the ribs

1. Remove the pouches from the water bath and allow them to sit at room temperature for 30 minutes. If not using immediately, cool in stages, submerging the pouches in cold water for an additional 30 minutes, and finally in an ice water bath for 1 hour. Refrigerate for up to 2 days.

2. When ready to finish, heat a grill or grill pan to high heat.

3. Remove the ribs from the pouches and sear the meat on the grill. Use the liquid in the pouches to baste the meat until a crust has developed and the interior of the meat is hot. Remove from the grill and allow the meat to rest for 5 minutes.

4. Present each rib portion on its own plate.

5. Garnish with celery salad and serve immediately.

1 tablespoon (15 ml) ground cumin

1 tablespoon (15 ml) ground turmeric

1 tablespoon (15 ml) ground black pepper

2 tablespoon (30 ml) kosher salt

4 beef short ribs, on the bone

For the celery salad

4 ribs celery

12 dates, pitted

40 parsley leaves

2 lemon, for juice

Kosher salt, to taste

beef rib roast

5 to 6 pound (2.2 to 2.7 kg) boneless beef rib roast

2 teaspoons garlic powder

2 teaspoons (.33 oz/9.6 g) coarse (kosher) salt

Freshly ground black pepper to taste

2 to 3 sprigs fresh rosemary

2 tablespoons (1 oz/30 g) clarified butter, melted

Serves 2
Cooking time: 8 to 10 hours

1. Fill and preheat the water oven to 134°F (56.5°C) for medium rare, 140°F (60°C) for medium.

2. Mix the seasonings together and sprinkle the mixture evenly over the surface of the meat.

3. Put the roast into a large (1 gallon/3.78 liter) cooking pouch, add the rosemary sprigs, and vacuum seal.

4. Submerge in the water oven and cook for 8 to 10 hours.

5. Remove the roast from the pouch, pat dry, and sear the surface of the meat, either in the clarified butter in a very hot skillet, or by brushing the surface with butter and searing under the broiler, or with a kitchen torch, to caramelize the exterior.

6. Slice and serve on warmed plates.

Asian short ribs

Serves 4
Cooking time: 72 hours

Make the glaze

1. Fill and preheat the water oven to 180°F (82°C).

2. In a small saucepan over medium heat, melt the sugar, stirring occasionally with a fork after it has begun to visibly melt. Cook until completely liquefied.

3. Stir in the ginger and set aside to cool slightly.

4. Meanwhile, in a small (1 quart/.9 liter) zip-closure cooking pouch, add all remaining ingredients.

5. Add the melted sugar to the pouch and stir to combine.

6. Evacuate the air from the pouch (page 11) and seal.

7. Submerge the pouch in the water oven and cook for 30 minutes. The food must be completely submerged to ensure even cooking.

8. Remove the pouch from the water oven and quick-chill, submerged in an ice water bath (half ice, half water), and store in the refrigerator for up to several weeks. Once you open the pouch, store any unused glaze, tightly capped, in a clean jar in the refrigerator.

Cook the ribs

1. Reset the temperature in the water bath to 134°F (56.5°C). To speed the process along, remove 1 to 2 quarts/liters of hot water from the water bath with a large measuring cup and replace it with an equivalent amount of ice water.

2. Lightly season the short ribs with salt and pepper.

3. Put the ribs into two small (1 quart/0.9 liter) cooking pouches and vacuum seal.

4. Submerge the pouches in the water oven and cook for 72 hours.

5. When ready to serve, heat a skillet, grill, or grill pan to high heat.

6. Remove the ribs from their pouches and pat dry.

7. Brush the Asian glaze over all surfaces of the ribs and sear on the high heat for 45 seconds per side.

8. Serve with additional glaze, if desired.

For the Asian barbecue glaze

$\frac{1}{3}$ cup (1.5 oz/43 g) brown sugar, lightly packed

1 inch (2.5 cm) fresh ginger root, peeled and minced

3 ounces (85 g) hoisin sauce

2 tablespoons (30 ml) unseasoned rice vinegar

1 tablespoon (15 ml) soy sauce

1 tablespoon (5 ml) nam pla (Asian fish sauce)

2 cloves garlic, peeled and minced

2 shallots, peeled and minced

$\frac{1}{8}$ teaspoon Chinese Five-spice powder

For the ribs

2 pounds (32 oz/0.9 kg) beef short ribs

Salt and pepper to taste

63

Balti beef

Serves 4
Cooking time: 8 to 12 hours

1. Fill and preheat the water oven to 134°F (56.5°C) for medium rare; 140°F (60°C) for medium; or 150°F (65.5°C) for medium-well.

2. Cut the red and green bell peppers and the onion into 1-inch (2.5 cm) chunks.

3. Heat the oil in a wok or frying pan over medium heat and sauté the cumin and fennel seeds until they begin to sputter. Stir in the curry paste and salt.

4. Add the garlic, ginger, Thai chili, peppers, and onion, and sauté for 5 minutes longer, until the vegetables begin to soften.

5. Put one piece of flank steak into each of two large (1 gallon/3.8 liter) cooking pouches, add half the vegetable mixture to each pouch, massage to coat, and vacuum seal.

6. Submerge the pouches in the water oven and cook for 8 to 12 hours.

7. After the cooking time has elapsed, heat sesame oil in a skillet over high heat until it reaches the smoking point.

8. Remove the flank steak from the pouches and sear for 30 seconds on each side.

9. Slice the steak into thin strips, put a portion on each plate, top with the vegetables from the pouch, and serve with Naan bread.

1 red bell pepper

1 green bell pepper

1 onion

1 tablespoon (15 ml) vegetable oil

1 teaspoon (5 ml) cumin seeds

$1/2$ teaspoon (2.5 ml) fennel seeds

1 tablespoon (15 ml) curry paste (hot or mild)

$1/2$ teaspoon (2.5 ml) salt

1 garlic clove, crushed

1-inch (2.5 cm) piece fresh ginger, peeled and minced

1 fresh red Thai chili, stemmed and finely chopped (remove seeds for less heat)

$1^1/2$ pounds (24 oz/675 g) flank steak, cut in half

1 tablespoon sesame oil

Naan bread, to serve

entrées

pork

baby back pork ribs

Courtesy of Sharone Hakman

Serves 4
Cooking time: 12 hours

Brine the pork

1. In a large pot, make the brine for the ribs by adding the kosher salt to the water and stirring until completely dissolved.

2. Divide the rib racks between two large (1 gallon/3.8 liter) zip-closure pouches. Pour half the brine into each pouch, and zip closed.

3. Refrigerate for several hours, up to overnight.

Cook the ribs

1. Fill and preheat the water oven to 150°F (65.5°C).

2. Remove the ribs from the brine, rinse, and pat dry.

3. In a bowl, make the seasoning mixture by whisking together all remaining ingredients, except the barbecue sauce.

4. Put each half of the rib racks into a large (1 gallon/3.8 liter) zip-closure cooking pouch, pour in one quarter of the seasoning mixture, evacuate the air from the pouch ((page 11) and zip closed.

5. Submerge the pouches in the water oven and cook for 12 hours. The food must be completely submerged to ensure even cooking.

6. Preheat a grill or oven broiler to high heat.

7. Remove the pouches from the water oven, open them, remove the racks, and pat the surface dry with paper towels.

8. Brush a generous amount of barbecue sauce over the surface and sear the ribs on the grill or under the broiler to caramelize the sauce.

9. Serve immediately with additional barbecue sauce and your favorite sides.

For the brine

$^1/_2$ gallon (64 oz/1.9 liters) water

$^1/_2$ cup (4 oz/120 g) kosher salt

2 racks baby back pork ribs, each cut in half

For the seasoning

$^1/_2$ cup (4 oz/120 ml) apple cider vinegar

$2^1/_2$ tablespoons (37.5 ml) brown sugar

1 cup (8 oz/240 ml) heavy, dark beer (Guinness works well)

$2^1/_2$ tablespoons (37.5 ml) honey

2 tablespoons (30 ml) paprika

1 bottle HAK's Barbecue Sauce (or your favorite brand)

stuffed pork tenderloin

Courtesy of Katherine Emmenegger, C.C.C.

Serves 6
Cooking time: 6 to 8 hours

1. Fill and preheat the water oven to 140°F (60°C).

2. In a skillet, over medium high heat, heat the oil and sauté the leek, shallots, and garlic until softened, about 5 minutes.

3. Add the thyme and parsley and sauté 2 minutes more.

4. Stir in the bread crumbs, salt, and pepper, and set aside to cool.

5. Trim the fat and remove the silver skin from the tenderloins, butterfly them, and pound out to an even thickness.

6. Season the pork with the salt and pepper on either side.

7. Spread the surfaces of the loins with the stuffing and roll in jelly-roll fashion.

8. Truss the pork with cotton kitchen twine.

9. Put each stuffed tenderloin into a cooking pouch and vacuum seal.

10. Submerge the food pouches in the water bath.

11. Cook at least 6 hours, but up to 8 hours will not affect the texture.

12. Remove the meat from the pouches, pat dry, and let stand for 5 minutes.

13. Sear for one minute per side over high heat on the grill or in a skillet.

14. Remove the kitchen twine, slice, and serve.

2 tablespoons (30 ml) olive oil

$1/2$ cup (1.5 oz/43 g) diced leeks, white part only, washed well

3 shallots, peeled and diced

2 large garlic cloves, peeled and minced

1 tablespoon (15 ml) minced fresh thyme leaves

$1/4$ cup (0.7 oz/19 g) minced fresh Italian parsley leaves

2 cups (3 oz/90 g) panko bread crumbs

Salt and pepper to taste

2 (1 lb/.45 kg each) pork tenderloins

pork belly sliders with slider slaw

Courtesy of Sharone Hakman

Serves 12
Cooking time: 10 to 18 hours

1. Fill and preheat the water oven to 176°F (80°C).

2. Put the pork belly, brown sugar, bourbon and crushed red pepper into a large (1 gallon/3.8 liter) cooking pouch and vacuum seal.

3. Submerge the pouch in the water oven and cook for at least 10 hours, but up to 18 hours will make the meat even more tender.

Meanwhile, make the Slider Slaw

1. In a bowl, whisk together the vinegar mayonnaise, sugar, lemon juice, salt and pepper until smooth.

2. Add the cabbage or slaw mix and toss to coat evenly.

3. Refrigerate until ready to use.

Finish the pork

1. Preheat a grill to medium heat.

2. Season the pork belly on both sides with salt and pepper to taste and grill the pork for 30 to 45 seconds per side to get a tasty crust all around.

3. Slice the pork belly and transfer to a warm platter.

Assemble the sliders

1. Lightly toast the slider buns,

2. Brush the bottom of each bun with barbecue sauce, if desired, and pile on the pork belly and Slider Slaw.

3. Top each with the other half-bun and serve.

For the sliders

2¹/₂ pounds (40 oz/1 kg) pork belly

¹/₄ cup (1 oz/31 g) brown sugar, lightly packed

1 tablespoon (15 ml) good bourbon

1 teaspoon (5 ml) crushed red chile pepper

Salt and pepper to taste

12 slider buns

For the slider slaw

1 tablespoon (15 ml) cider vinegar

3 tablespoons (45 ml) prepared mayonnaise

2 teaspoons (10 ml) sugar

1 lemon, juice only

Salt and pepper to taste

2 cups (24 oz/680 g) shredded cabbage or cabbage slaw mix

Black sesame seeds for garnish

the perfect pork chop

Serves 1 to 4
Cooking time: 4 to 8 hours

For best results, brine the pork chops

1. Dissolve the kosher salt in the water in a large (1 gallon/3.8 liter) zip-closure bag or covered container.

2. Put the chops into the brine, seal or cover, and refrigerate for 4 hours or up to overnight.

Cook the pork chops

1. Fill and preheat the water oven to 134°F (56.5°C) for medium-rare; 140°F (60°C) for medium; or 160°F (71°C) for medium-well.

2. Remove the chops from the brine and discard the brining liquid. Rinse the chops in cold water and pat dry.

3. Sprinkle the chops lightly on both sides with each of the seasonings, omitting the salt if the chops have been brined.

4. Put one or two seasoned chops, along with a generous tablespoon of bacon fat or butter, if desired, into each cooking pouch and vacuum seal.

5. Submerge the pouch(es) in the water oven and cook for at least 4 hours, and up to 8 hours.

Finish the chops

1. Remove the chops from the cooking pouch(es) and pat dry with paper towels.

2. On the stove top, put the butter, rosemary, and garlic into a skillet over medium high heat. When the butter foams, sear the chops for approximately 1 minute on each side to a golden brown.

3. Put each chop onto a warmed plate and pour some browned butter from the skillet over it.

For the brine
1/4 cup (2 oz/60 g) kosher salt
1 quart (32 oz/946 ml) water

For the chops
1 to 4 double thick boneless pork chops (about 2-inches/5-cm thick)
Coarse salt
Freshly ground black pepper
Garlic powder
Onion powder
Paprika
1 to 4 tablespoons (15 to 60 ml) bacon fat or butter (optional)

For finishing
2 tablespoons (30 ml) unsalted butter
1 sprig fresh rosemary
1 clove garlic, peeled and smashed

lentil soup with sausage

1 cup (6 oz/177 g) green lentils

1 small red pepper, finely diced

1 green pepper, finely diced

1 small onion, finely diced

2 tablespoons (30 ml) fennel seeds

1 tablespoon (30 ml)
ground coriander

1 tablespoon (30 ml) ground cumin

3 cups (24 oz/710 ml)
chicken broth

Salt and freshly ground pepper
to taste

4 sweet Italian sausages in
their casings

16 baby carrots

Freshly grated Parmesan cheese,
for serving

Serves 4
Cooking time: 3 to 6 hours

Cook the lentils

1. Fill and preheat the water oven to 195°F (90.5°C).

2. Combine the lentils, peppers, onions, spices, and chicken broth in
two large (1 gallon/3.8 liter) zip-closure cooking pouches. Evacuate
the air from the pouches (page 11) and zip closed.

3. Submerge the pouches in the water oven and cook for at least
3 hours and up to 6 hours.

Cook the sausages and carrots

1. Vacuum seal the sausages in a small (1 quart/.9 liter) cooking pouch.

2. Vacuum seal the carrots in a small (1 quart/.9 liter) cooking pouch.

3. A half-hour before serving, submerge the sausage and carrot
pouches in the water oven and cook for 30 minutes.

Assemble the soup

1. Remove the sausage from the cooking pouch, slice into one-eight-inch (0.32-cm) pieces, and divide among
4 bowls.

2. Remove the carrots from the cooking pouch and divide among the bowls.

3. Spoon the lentil soup mixture into the serving bowls. Add salt and freshly ground pepper to taste, and serve
with grated Parmesan cheese.

barbecue ribs with sweet corn tomalito

Courtesy of Katherine Emmenegger, C.C.C.

Serves 4
Cooking time: 8 to 12 hours

1. Fill and preheat the water oven to 160°–176°F (71°–80°C).

2. Season the pork ribs with salt, pepper, and chili powder.

3. In a skillet, over high heat, heat the oil and sear the pork to brown on each side, about 30 seconds. Set the pork ribs aside.

4. In the same pan, sauté the onions, peppers, and garlic until lightly browned; about 1 to 2 minutes.

5. Add all remaining ingredients and bring to a simmer. Pour the sauce over the pork.

6. Transfer the ribs into a large (1 gallon/3.8 liter) zip-closure cooking pouch. Evacuate the air from the pouch (page 11) and zip closed.

7. Submerge the pouch in the water oven and cook for 8 to 12 hours. The food must be submerged completely for even cooking.

Make the Sweet Corn Tomalito ahead of time, or with the ribs if cooking at the same temperature

1. Fill and preheat the water oven to 176°F (80°C).

2. In a bowl, combine all ingredients.

3. Put the corn mixture into a large (1 gallon/3.8 liter) zip-closure cooking pouch. Evacuate the air from the pouch (page 11) and zip closed.

4. Submerge the pouch in the water bath and cook for 2 to 8 hours. It must be submerged completely to ensure even cooking.

Plating

1. Remove the ribs from the pouch and transfer to a warm plate.

2. Remove the tomalito from the pouch and serve with the pork ribs.

For the ribs

1 teaspoon (5 ml) salt

½ teaspoon (2.5 ml) black pepper

1 tablespoon (15 ml) chile powder

2 tablespoons (30 ml) vegetable oil

2 pounds (32 0z/0.91 kg) boneless country style pork ribs, rinsed and patted dry with a paper towel

1 yellow onion, peeled and julienned

1 red bell pepper, washed, cored, and julienned

3 garlic cloves, peeled and minced

1 (12 oz/340 g) bottle Heinz Chili Sauce

½ cup (4 oz/120 ml) water

3 tablespoons (45 ml) red wine vinegar

1 teaspoon (5 ml) Worcestershire sauce

2 teaspoons (10 ml) Dijon mustard

2 teaspoons (10 ml) chili powder

½ teaspoon (2.5 ml) celery seed

3 tablespoons (45 ml) brown sugar

Salt and pepper to taste

For the sweet corn tomalito

½ cup (2.5 oz/125 g) cornmeal

¼ cup (1.3 oz/37.5 g) masa harina

1 teaspoon (5 ml) baking powder

½ teaspoon (2.5 ml) salt

1 cup (8 oz/230 g) fresh corn cut from the cob (about 2 medium ears) or frozen whole-kernel corn, thawed

½ cup (4 oz/120 ml) whole milk

5 tablespoons (75 ml) softened, unsalted butter or vegetable shortening

⅓ cup (2.4 oz/67 g) granulated sugar

sous vide tamales

Courtesy of Katherine Emmenegger, C.C.C.

Makes 36 tamales
Cooking time: 8 to 10 hours for the filling,
plus 2 to 6 hours for the tamales

1. Fill and preheat the water oven to 134°F (56.5°C).

2. Rinse the pork, pat it dry, and cut the meat into approximately ¼-pound (4 oz/113 g) chunks.

3. Season the pork with the salt, pepper, and chili powder to taste.

4. Divide the pork, onions, garlic, and broth evenly between two large (1 gallon/3.8 liter) zip-closure cooking pouches. Evacuate the air from the pouches (page 11), and zip closed.

5. Put the pouches into the water bath, making sure the pouches are completely submerged to ensure even cooking.

6. Cook for 8 to 10 hours.

7. Remove the pork from the pouches to a sheet tray to cool.

8. Remove any visible fat and shred the meat.

Make the red sauce

1. In a saucepan, over medium heat, heat the oil and sauté the onions and garlic for 3 to 4 minutes.

2. Add the tomato purée, cumin, ancho chile powder, and oregano, and simmer for 20 minutes.

3. Adjust the seasonings with salt and cayenne pepper and let cool.

4. Mix the red sauce with the shredded meat, and follow the directions for tamale preparation and cooking. The sauce may be stored in the refrigerator in an airtight container for up to 3 days.

Make the masa

1. In a deep bowl, combine the masa, baking powder, and salt, and mix well.

2. Pour the broth into the masa a little at a time, working it in with your fingers.

For the spicy pork filling

4 pounds (1.81 kg) pork shoulder, bone in, (Boston Butt)

Salt, pepper, and chile powder, to taste

2 large yellow onions, peeled and julienned

4 garlic cloves, peeled and crushed

2 cups (16 oz/473 ml) vegetable broth

For the red sauce

2 tablespoons (30 ml) vegetable oil

1 large yellow onion, peeled and diced small

2 garlic cloves, peeled and minced

1 can (28 oz/828 g) tomato purée

2 tablespoons (30 ml) ground cumin or to taste

3 tablespoons (45 ml) ancho chile powder or to taste

1 tablespoon (15 ml) dried oregano, crumbled, or to taste

Salt and cayenne pepper, to taste

For the masa

4 cups (20 oz/600 g) packed dry masa mix

1 tablespoon (15 ml) baking powder, best if fresh

2 teaspoons (10 ml) salt

4 cups (32 oz/946 ml) beef, chicken, or vegetable broth

1⅓ cups (9.3 oz/264 g) lard or vegetable shortening

For the tamales

2 bags of corn husks

For serving

Salsa

Sour cream

Cilantro

sous vide tamales

continued from page 79

3. In a large bowl, use an electric mixer, fitted with the paddle attachment if you have it, to whip the lard or shortening until fluffy; add the masa and combine until just mixed.

Assemble and cook the tamales

1. Fill and preheat the water oven to 176°F (80°C).

2. Soak the corn husks in hot water for 1 hour.

3. Remove the silk.

4. Rinse the husks and drain well.

5. Using the largest husks, lay them flat on a plate or work surface with the smooth side up and the narrow end facing you.

6. Scoop 3 tablespoons (45 ml) of the masa onto a husk; lay a piece of plastic wrap over the masa and press with your palm to flatten. Remove the plastic wrap and use for the remaining tamales.

7. Put about 2 to 3 tablespoons (30 to 45 ml) of pork filling down the center of the masa, bring the long sides of the husk together to encase the filling in masa, fold the bottom of the husk up, and roll the husk from the bottom, but not too tightly.

8. Arrange the rolled tamales evenly in two large (1 gallon/3.8 liter) zip-closure cooking pouches, in no more than two layers.

9. Evacuate the air from the pouches (page 11), and zip closed.

10. Submerge the pouches in the water bath and cook for 2 to 6 hours. The food must be submerged completely to ensure even cooking.

11. Carefully open the pouches and remove the tamales. The tamales are done when the masa pulls cleanly away from the husk. The tamale should be soft, yet firm and not mushy.

12. Serve with accompaniments such as salsas, sour cream, and cilantro.

risotto with ham and mushrooms

Serves 4
Cooking time: 45 minutes

1. Fill and preheat the water oven to 183°F (84°C).

2. Evenly divide the rice, pancetta, mushrooms and broth between two small (1 quart/.9 liter) zip-closure cooking pouches, evacuate the air (page 11) and zip closed.

3. Submerge the pouches in the water oven and cook for 45 minutes. The food must be completely submerged to ensure even cooking.

4. Remove the pouches promptly after 45 minutes, let them rest for 5 minutes, and then put the contents into a mixing bowl.

5. Stir in the Parmesan cheese, salt, and freshly grated pepper. Stir in the cream, if using, divide among four bowls, and serve.

1 cup (3 oz/90 g) arborio rice

$\frac{1}{2}$ tablespoon (7.5 ml) butter

3 cups (24 oz/710 ml) chicken broth

$\frac{1}{2}$ cup (2 oz/59 g) cubed pancetta

8 crimini mushrooms, sliced

$\frac{1}{4}$ cup (.9 oz/25 g) freshly grated Parmesan cheese

Salt and freshly ground pepper to taste

$\frac{1}{8}$ cup (2 oz/59 ml) cream (optional)

entrées

lamb

83

 sous vide lamb video

scan the code with your smart phone,
or visit sousvidesupreme.com/thecookbook

Mediterranean lamb shanks

Courtesy of Katherine Emmenegger, C.C.C.

Serves 4
Cooking time: 12 to 30 hours

1. Fill and preheat the water oven to 160–176°F (71–80°C).

2. Caramelize the surface of the lamb shanks in a 400°F (204°C) oven, turning regularly, or brown with a kitchen torch.

3. In a bowl, combine the wine and flour and mix to a smooth consistency.

4. Divide ingredients evenly between two large (1 gallon/3.8 liter) zip-closure cooking pouches, evacuate the air from the pouches (page 11), and zip closed.

5. Submerge the pouches in the water oven, and cook for 12 to 30 hours. The food must be submerged completely to ensure even cooking.

6. During the last hour of cooking, open the pouches, add the orzo pasta to each pouch, reseal, and return to the water bath.

7. When ready, remove the pouches, carefully open them, and arrange the shanks and orzo on serving plates.

8. Garnish with a sprig of rosemary.

4 lamb shanks

1 medium yellow onion, peeled and diced medium

2 large garlic cloves, peeled and minced

1 can (28 oz/794 g) diced tomatoes

1/2 cup (4 oz/120 ml) dry red wine

2 tablespoons (2 ml) all-purpose flour

2 teaspoons (10 ml) dry oregano

Salt and pepper, to taste

1/2 cup (3.5 oz/99 g) orzo pasta

Fresh rosemary, for garnish

rack of lamb with mint sauce

Serves 4
Cooking time: 1½ to 4 hours

1. Fill and preheat the water oven to 134°F (56.5°C).

2. Sprinkle both sides of the racks or chops liberally with salt and pepper.

3. Put each lamb rack (or 3 to 4 chops) into a small (1 quart/.9 liter) cooking pouch and vacuum seal.

4. Submerge the food pouches in the water bath and cook for at least 1½ hours (but up to 4 hours will not affect the texture of the meat.)

Make the mint sauce

1. Whisk all ingredients together in a small bowl.

2. Let the sauce sit at room temperature for 15 to 20 minutes to allow flavors to blend.

Finish the lamb

1. At the end of the lamb's cooking time, melt the butter and combine with all remaining herbed butter ingredients.

2. When ready to serve, remove the lamb from the pouches, pat the surface dry, and brush all over with the herbed butter mixture.

3. Sear the lamb quickly on one side in a hot skillet or for about 3 minutes under the broiler. (Sear the rack meaty side down in the skillet or meaty side up under the broiler.)

4. Slice the rack into chops and top with mint sauce, if desired.

2 lamb racks, Frenched
(or 12 meaty t-bone lamb chops)

Salt and pepper to taste

For the herbed butter

2 tablespoons (30 ml) butter

1 clove garlic, peeled and pressed

½ teaspoon (2.5 ml) onion powder

1 teaspoon (5 ml) fresh rosemary leaves, minced

1 tablespoon (15 ml) grated Parmesan

For the mint sauce

2 tablespoons (30 ml) fresh mint leaves, minced

⅓ cup (2.6 oz/77 ml) apple cider or red wine vinegar

2 teaspoons (10 ml) sugar
(or 1 packet sweetener)

Irish lamb stew

Serves 6
Cooking time: 8 to 10 hours

1. Fill and preheat the water oven to 185°F (80°C).

2. Put 2 tablespoons (60 ml) of the olive oil into a skillet over medium high heat.

3. When hot, add the stew meat and sear quickly on all sides to brown the surface; remove meat to a large bowl and set aside.

4. Add the remaining olive oil and the butter to the skillet and heat until the butter has melted.

5. Add the garlic and cook briefly, but do not brown.

6. Sprinkle in the flour to make a roux, whisking continuously for about 2 minutes.

7. Add 2 to 3 cups (16 to 24 oz/473 to 710 ml) of the beef stock and continue to whisk until the pan liquids reach the thickness you prefer for the stew. Add more or less liquid to your liking.

8. Add all vegetables and herbs to the sauce in the bowl and mix well.

9. Divide the vegetables, including the pan liquid, evenly between two large (1 gallon/3.8 liter) zip-closure cooking pouches. Evacuate the air from the pouches (page 11), and zip closed.

10. Submerge the pouches in the water oven to cook for 1 hour.

11. Meanwhile, put the lamb in a single layer into a large (1 gallon/3.8 liter) cooking pouch and refrigerate while the vegetables cook.

12. When the vegetables have cooked, remove the pouches and quick chill, submerged in an ice water bath (half ice, half water). Refrigerate the vegetables in their pouches.

13. Reset the temperature of the water oven to 140°F (60°). Remove some hot water and add ice and water to speed up the cooling process.

14. Submerge the pouch of lamb in the water oven to cook for 8 to 10 hours. During the last 30 minutes to 1 hour, return the vegetable pouches to the water oven to reheat alongside the lamb.

15. When ready, pour the vegetables, sauce, and lamb into a serving dish. Remove or discard any herb stalks.

16. Ladle the stew into bowls and top each serving with a dollop of sour cream or crème fraîche.

4 tablespoons (60 ml) extra virgin olive oil, divided use

2 pounds (0.91 kg) lamb stew meat, cut into 1-inch (2.5-cm) chunks

2 tablespoons (30 ml) unsalted butter

2 tablespoons (30 ml) minced garlic

4 tablespoons (60 ml) flour

1 quart (32 oz/946 ml) beef stock

$1\frac{1}{2}$ pounds (24 oz/710 g) baby Yukon gold or red new potatoes, halved

1 pound (16 oz/473 g) baby carrots (about one bag)

1 cup (4 oz/110 g) frozen or fresh green peas

2 cans (28 oz/828 g) stewed tomatoes

4 sprigs fresh thyme

1 sprigs fresh rosemary

2 whole sprigs fresh mint

Sour cream or crème fraîche for garnish

shepherd's pie

Serves 4
Cooking time: 7.5 to 10 hours

1. Fill and preheat the water oven to 134°F (56.5°C) for medium-rare, 140°F (60°C) for medium.

2. Put the stew meat into a bowl, add the seasonings, and toss to coat the meat.

3. Heat the oil in a skillet over medium-high heat until shimmering.

4. Brown the meat on all sides in the hot oil. Remove from the skillet and allow the meat to cool.

5. Sprinkle the flour into the hot skillet and stir to brown slightly.

6. Deglaze the skillet with the beef broth, stirring as the pan sauce thickens. Taste for seasonings and add a bit more salt or pepper to your taste, if desired.

7. Remove the sauce from the heat and allow it to cool. Then pour the pan sauce into a zip-closure cooking pouch, evacuate the air from the pouch (page 11), and zip closed. Refrigerate until it's time to reheat the meat before assembling the pie.

8. Put the browned meat in a single layer into a large (1 gallon/3.8 liter) cooking pouch, and vacuum seal.

9. Submerge the meat fully in the water bath, and cook for 6 to 8 hours. At this point, you may continue with the recipe, or quick chill the pouch by submerging it in ice water for at least 30 minutes, and then refrigerate it for up to 48 hours.

Cook the vegetables

1. Fill and preheat (or raise the temperature of) the water oven to 183°F (84°C).

2. Cut the cauliflower in half, then into ½-inch (1.3 cm) slices.

3. Put cauliflower into a large (1 gallon/3.8 liter) cooking pouch, along with the butter. Sprinkle with salt and pepper and vacuum seal the pouch.

4. Put the onions and the carrots into another cooking pouch, sprinkle with salt and pepper, and vacuum seal.

For the meat

1 pound (16 oz/0.45 kg) beef or lamb stew meat, cut into 1-inch (2.5-cm) cubes

1 teaspoon (5 ml) coarse salt

½ teaspoon (2.5 ml) black pepper

¼ teaspoon (1.25 ml) garlic powder

¼ teaspoon (1.25 ml) onion powder

2 tablespoons (30 ml) olive oil

2 tablespoons (30 ml) all-purpose flour

1 cup (8 oz/240 ml) beef broth

For the vegetables

1 small head cauliflower, washed and trimmed

2 tablespoons (60 ml) butter

Salt and pepper to taste

10 to 12 pearl onions, peeled

2 carrots, peeled and cut into 2-inch (5 cm) pieces

¼ cup (2 oz/60 ml) heavy cream

5. Put the pouches in the water oven and cook for at least and hour and up to 90 minutes. The vegetables must be submerged completely to ensure even cooking.

6. When the vegetables are cooked, reset the temperature in the water bath to 134°F (56.5°C). To speed the process along, remove 1 to 2 quarts/liters of hot water from the water bath with a large measuring cup and replace it with an equivalent amount of ice water.

7. When the temperature stabilizes at 134°F (56.5°C), return the meat and sauce pouches to the water bath, and let them come to temperature (about 30 minutes).

Assemble the pie

1. Preheat the broiler to high.

2. Remove the pouches from the water oven, open each pouch, and drain away the liquid from the pouches of meat and vegetables.

3. Pour the cooked cauliflower into the work bowl of a food processor or a blender jar, add ¼ cup (2 oz/60 ml) heavy cream and purée until smooth. Taste for seasonings and adjust with salt and pepper to your liking.

4. In a deep casserole dish, combine the meat, onions, carrots, and pan sauce and toss to coat evenly.

5. Top with the cauliflower purée, and spread it evenly over the pie.

6. Put the casserole under the broiler to lightly brown the top.

7. Serve immediately.

lamb shanks with Bengali potatoes

Courtesy of Chef Sam Hussain

Serves 4
Cooking time: 49 hours

Marinate the meat

1. Mix the yogurt, mint paste, black pepper, paprika and cumin in a large bowl. Add the lamb shanks and turn to coat them completely with the marinade.

2. Cover the bowl with plastic wrap (cling film) and marinate in the refrigerator overnight.

Cook the lamb shanks

1. Fill and preheat the water oven to 140°F (60°C).

2. Remove the lamb shanks from the marinade and wipe away the excess. Put each shank into a separate cooking pouch and vacuum seal.

3. Submerge the pouches in the water bath and cook for 48 hours.

4. Remove the pouches from the water oven and put them in a large pot filled with hottest tap water and cover to keep warm while preparing the Bengali potatoes.

Prepare the Bengali potatoes

1. Raise the temperature of the water oven to 182°F (83°C).

2. Peel the potatoes and coarsely chop them.

3. Put the potatoes in an even layer in a cooking pouch and vacuum seal.

4. Submerge the pouch in the water oven to cook for 30 to 45 minutes, until tender.

5. Remove the potatoes from the pouch and drain any liquid.

6. Transfer the potatoes to a large bowl and mash them coarsely.

7. Add the remaining ingredients and mix well. Keep hot for serving.

For the marinade

7 ounces (200 g) full-fat natural yogurt

1 teaspoon (5 ml) mint paste

1/2 teaspoon (2.5 ml) ground black pepper

1 teaspoon (5 ml) paprika

1 tablespoon (15 ml) cumin seeds

4 lamb shanks, rinsed and scored

For Bengali-style mashed potatoes

4 or 5 large russet potatoes (or other suitable varieties for mashing)

2 red onions, peeled and finely chopped

2 green chile peppers, stemmed, seeded, and chopped

Small handful coriander leaves, chopped

1 teaspoon (5 ml) mustard oil

1/2 teaspoon (2.5 ml) salt

1/2 teaspoon (2.5 ml) red chili powder

1/2 teaspoon (2.5 ml) cumin seeds

For coconut milk sauce

2 large onions, peeled and coarsely chopped

2 tablespoons (30 ml) olive oil

Pinch of salt

1 teaspoon (5 ml) ginger garlic paste

3 tablespoons (45 ml) curry paste

1 can (14 ounces/400 g) chopped tomatoes

2 2/3 cups (22 oz/650 ml) chicken stock, heated

2/3 cup (5 oz/150 ml) coconut milk

For plating

Fresh cilantro (coriander) leaves, roughly chopped

3 or 4 chive stems for garnish

lamb shanks with Bengali potatoes

continued from page 91

Make the coconut milk sauce

1. Put the onion into a food processor fitted with a steel blade and process to a paste.

2. Heat oil in large skillet or casserole, add the onion paste and when slightly brown add the salt and stir for a minute.

3. Stir in the ginger garlic paste and let it brown slightly, then add the curry paste.

4. Increase the heat and cook, stirring, for a couple of minutes more.

5. Pour in the tomatoes, stock and coconut milk and bring to the boil. Cover with a lid, and cook slowly until the sauce has thickened.

6. Remove the shanks from the cooking pouch and put them in the pan with the sauce, coat them with it, and let them warm for a few minutes.

7. Serve with Bengali-style mashed potatoes. Spoon on additional sauce and sprinkle fresh coriander and chives over the plate to finish the dish.

fig-mint of lamb with pea soup

Courtesy of Chef Phillip Foss

Serves 4
Cooking time: 1 hour

1. Trim the stems from the figs, mint and parsley.

2. In a blender or food processor, purée the figs, herbs, half the water, the vinegar, brown sugar and black pepper.

3. Add the rest of the water and continue to process a minute or so more.

4. Taste the marinade. It should have notes of sweetness, acidity from the vinegar and a good dose of spice from the black pepper. Adjust the seasoning to your liking.

5. Put the lamb into a small (1 quart/0.9 liter) zip-closure cooking pouch, cover with the marinade, evacuate the air from the pouch (page 11) and zip closed.

6. Marinate overnight in the refrigerator.

7. Fill and preheat the water oven to 134°F (56.5°C) for medium-rare.

8. Submerge the pouch in the water bath and cook for 1 hour.

Prepare the pea soup

1. Bring a large pot of salted water to a boil and blanch the peas until tender (about 3 minutes).

2. Transfer to an ice bath, cool completely, and drain. (If using frozen peas, thaw completely before continuing.)

3. Put the peas in a blender and add the cold chicken stock. Blend over high speed until very smooth (about 3 minutes).

Prepare the leeks

1. Thoroughly wash the diced leeks, rinse well to remove all grit, and dry them.

2. Heat the olive oil over medium heat in a non-reactive, heavy-gauge sauce pan large enough to comfortably fit the leeks without overcrowding and without excessive spacing.

3. Add the leeks, season with salt, and cook until the water has cooked out.

4. If not serving immediately, spread the leeks out over as much surface as possible to cool.

8 ounces (226 g) dried figs

$^{1}/_{4}$ bunch fresh mint

$^{1}/_{4}$ bunch Italian parsley

$2^{1}/_{2}$ cups (20 oz/591 ml) water

2 tablespoons (30 ml) balsamic vinegar

2 tablespoons (30 ml) brown sugar

$1^{1}/_{2}$ tablespoons (22.5 ml) freshly ground black pepper

1 rack of lamb, tenderloin removed from the bone (or left on the rack, if desired, and sliced into portions at plating)

Salt and pepper, to taste

For the pea soup

4 cups (20.5 oz/580 g) shucked, fresh peas (substitute with frozen)

$1^{1}/_{2}$ cups (12 oz/340 ml) chicken stock

Salt, to taste

For the braised leeks

8 cups (25 oz/712 g) leeks, diced large

$^{1}/_{2}$ cup (4 oz/120 ml) extra virgin olive oil

Salt, to taste

fig-mint of lamb with pea soup

continued from page 93

Finish the lamb and plate

1. Preheat an oiled charcoal grill or grill pan to high heat.

2. Remove the lamb from the pouch and wipe off excess marinade.

3. Cut the lamb tenderloin into four uniform pieces (or the rack into chops). Season lightly with salt and fresh cracked black pepper.

4. Sear the lamb quickly on all sides, and transfer to a wire rack to rest for 1 to 2 minutes before serving.

5. Season the pea soup to taste, and bring to a boil.

6. Spoon the leeks into the center of four warm bowls and position the lamb portions on top.

7. Pour the hot pea soup around the lamb and serve.

rack of lamb with vegetables

Courtesy of Chef John Loydall

Serves 2
Cooking time: 2½ hours

Cook the vegetables

1. Fill and preheat the water oven to 183°F (84°C).

2. Put all the vegetables, except the beans, into a large cooking pouch. Season to taste with salt and pepper and vacuum seal.

3. Submerge the pouch in the water oven and cook for 1 hour.

Start the sauce

1. In a pan gently sweat the onion, celery, leek and carrots in a tablespoon of oil until softened, about 15 minutes. Don't allow the mixture to brown too much.

2. Add the lamb stock, bay, thyme, star anise and peppercorns and continue to cook for 1 hour over a low flame. Don't allow it to boil.

3. When the vegetables have been cooking in the water oven for 30 minutes, in a pan on the stove top, fry the shallots until softened.

4. Add the wine to the shallots and reduce over a low heat for 30 minutes.

Cook the lamb

1. When the vegetables in the water oven have been cooking for 1 hour, reset the temperature of the water oven to140°F (60°C). (Add cold water or ice to hasten the drop.) Leave the vegetable pouches in the water bath to keep them warm.

2. Put the lamb and its herbs and seasonings into a cooking pouch and vacuum seal.

3. Submerge the lamb alongside the vegetables and cook for 1 hour.

Cook the beans and finish the sauce

1. Bring a pot of water to a boil on the stove top and cook the beans until tender.

For the vegetables

3 carrots, peeled and sliced lengthwise

4 shallots peeled and quartered

2 baby leeks, trimmed and sliced

1 baby cauliflower, separated into florets

½ teaspoon (2.5 ml) each salt and ground black pepper

For the sauce

1 tablespoon (15 ml) olive oil

1 onion, peeled and chopped

1 rib (stick) celery, chopped

1 leek, trimmed and chopped

2 carrots, peeled and chopped

3 cups (24 oz/720 ml) lamb stock

1 bay leaf

3 sprigs thyme, picked

3 star anise

15 whole black peppercorns

3 shallots, peeled and chopped

½ bottle (12.5 oz/375 ml) red wine

For the lamb

1 rack of lamb (allow 2 to 3 chops per person)

2 bay leaves

2 sprigs rosemary

4 sprigs thyme

Salt and black pepper to taste

For the beans

½ cup (3 oz/85 g) broad (fava) beans

½ cup (3 oz/85 g) flageolet beans

rack of lamb
with vegetables

continued from page 97

2. While the lamb and beans are cooking, strain the lamb stock into the pan with the shallots and red wine and reduce further, about 30 minutes. Don't allow it to boil.

3. Strain the sauce to remove the shallots and skim any froth from the surface. Return to the pan and reduce further for another 30 minutes.

4. Taste the sauce and adjust the seasonings to your taste. If you want to sweeten the sauce, consider a teaspoon or two of red currant jelly. When it tastes and looks good, it's ready to go.

Finish the lamb and plate

1. When the lamb has cooked, remove the pouch from the water, open it, and pat the lamb dry.

2. Heat a pan on the stove top to high heat and sear the lamb on all sides for a minute or two to add some color and texture to the surface of the meat.

3. To serve, put the vegetables (straight from the pouch) and beans onto the plate. Cut the rack of lamb into chops and arrange over the vegetables. Top with the sauce.

lamb belly with Turkish spice

Courtesy of Chef Michael Solomonov

Serves 4
Cooking time: 36 hours

1. Fill and preheat the water oven to 145°F (63°C).

2. In a small bowl, combine all the spices, season the lamb bellies all over with the mixture, cover, and refrigerate for 12 hours.

3. Remove the lamb bellies from the refrigerator, sprinkle one surface of each belly with the transglutaminase, and press two bellies together to form a single, thicker "lamb steak." Wrap the steak with microwave-safe plastic wrap (cling film) and refrigerate for another hour to bond.

4. Put each plastic-wrapped (cling-film-wrapped) steak into a small (1 quart/0.9 liter) cooking pouch and vacuum seal.

5. Submerge the pouches in the water bath and cook for 36 hours.

6. Remove the pouches and cool in an ice bath (half ice, half water) for 45 minutes to 1 hour, replenishing ice as needed. Refrigerate for up to 48 hours if not proceeding immediately.

7. When ready to finish, heat a pan or plancha to high heat, remove the lamb from the pouch, remove and discard the plastic wrap (cling film), and sear the lamb until both sides are well browned.

Chef's recommended plating

1. Slice each lamb steak into four long pieces.

2. Plate each slice with a little dressed lettuce or chopped cucumber.

1 teaspoon (5 ml) ground cinnamon

1 teaspoon (5 ml) ground black pepper

1 teaspoon (5ml) ground coriander

1 teaspoon (5 ml) ground urfa (or cayenne) pepper

Kosher salt to taste

2 (8-oz/240-g) lamb bellies, cut in half

1 teaspoon (5 ml) transglutaminase

Transglutaminase is a naturally occurring enzyme, often referred to as "meat glue" for its property to bind proteins together. It is sold commercially as Activa® and available through restaurant suppliers or on amazon.com.

For plating

Dressed lettuce or chopped cucumber

entrées

sage turkey breast video

scan the code with your smart phone,
or visit sousvidesupreme.com/thecookbook

barbecue chicken leg quarters

Serves 4
Cooking time: 4 to 6 hours

Brine the chicken

1. In a large (1 gallon/3.8 liter) zip-closure bag, make a brining solution by dissolving the salt in the water.

2. Add the chicken, zip the bag closed, and refrigerate overnight.

Cook the chicken

1. Fill and preheat the water oven to 176°F (80°C).

2. Remove the chicken from the brine, rinse, and pat dry.

3. Mix the ingredients for the rub in a small bowl.

4. Season the chicken on all sides with the rub.

5. Put each leg quarter into a small (1 quart/0.9 liter) cooking pouch and vacuum seal.

6. Submerge the pouches in the water oven and cook for 4 to 6 hours.

7. Before serving, heat an oiled grill to high heat.

8. Remove the chicken from the pouches, pat dry, and sear on the grill to add grill marks and flavor.

For the brine
$^1/_2$ gallon (64 oz./1.9 liter) water
$^1/_2$ cup (4 oz/120g) kosher salt
4 chicken leg quarters

For the seasoning rub
2 tablespoons (30 ml) paprika
1 tablespoon (15 ml) chile powder
1 teaspoon (5 ml) onion powder
1 teaspoon (5 ml) garlic powder
1 teaspoon (5 ml) black pepper
$^1/_4$ teaspoon (1.25 ml) cayenne pepper

chicken dockside

Courtesy of Pam McKinstry

Serves 4
Cooking time 1 to 3 hours

1. Fill and preheat the water oven to 146°F (63.5°C).

2. Fill a medium-size bowl with ice and water and set aside.

3. Bring a small saucepan of water to a boil over high heat and add the carrots and blanche for 30 seconds. Add the leeks to the boiling water and continue to cook an additional 30 seconds. (The zucchini is not blanched.)

4. Drain the vegetables and plunge them into the prepared ice bath.

5. When cool, drain again thoroughly and set them aside.

6. In a small bowl, mash the butter with a spoon until it is smooth.

7. Add 1 tablespoon of the tarragon to the butter and mix together to make a paste. Set aside at room temperature.

8. Trim the chicken, discarding fat and tendons. Remove the tenderloins (if any) from the breasts and reserve for another purpose.

9. Put one breast at a time into a zip-closure bag or between sheets of parchment or wax paper, and lightly pound to an even thickness of ¼ inch (0.6 cm.)

10. Season each breast with salt and pepper.

11. Put one chicken breast on a clean work surface and arrange a small, neat bundle of julienned carrots, leeks, and zucchini at the end nearest you. Add a tablespoon of the tarragon butter atop the vegetables.

12. Starting at the end with the vegetables, roll the chicken tightly around the vegetable bundle, and secure with a toothpick or kitchen twine. Repeat with the remaining breasts and vegetables. (Reserve any leftover julienned vegetables for the sauce.)

13. Put the chicken rolls into one or more cooking pouches and vacuum seal. (Pouches may be prepared ahead of time and refrigerated for up to 2 days before cooking.)

14. Submerge the pouch(es) in the water bath and cook for 1 hour, and up to 3 hours.

1 large carrot, trimmed, peeled, and cut julienne in 2½-inch (6-cm) lengths

1 large leek, white and light green parts, cut julienne in 2½-inch (6-cm) lengths

1 large zucchini, trimmed and cut julienne in 2½-inch (6-cm) lengths

½ stick (2 oz/59 g) unsalted butter, softened

2 tablespoons (30 ml) minced fresh tarragon, divided use

4 (6-oz/180-g each) boneless, skinless chicken breast halves

Kosher or sea salt

Freshly ground black pepper

For the sauce

2 cups (16 oz/473 ml) good quality chicken stock

¼ cup (2 oz/59 ml) dry vermouth or white wine

⅔ cup (5 oz/153 g) créme fraîche

1 tablespoon (15 ml) minced fresh flat-leaf parsley

chicken dockside

continued from page 105

Make the sauce

1. In a small skillet over medium heat, reduce the chicken stock to ¾ cup.

2. Add the vermouth and continue to cook for 5 minutes.

3. Reduce the heat to low, add the créme fraîche, and continue to cook, stirring frequently, until the sauce thickens, about 10 minutes.

4. Add the remaining julienned carrots, leeks, zucchini, parsley, and the remaining tarragon to the sauce and heat through. Season to taste with salt and pepper, and keep the sauce warm until ready to serve.

5. If the sauce is prepared ahead of serving time, pour it into a zip-closure cooking pouch, evacuate the air (page 11), zip the pouch closed and submerge it in the warm water oven with the chicken until needed.

6. When ready to serve, take the chicken from the pouch and remove any twine or toothpicks. Cut each roll crosswise (sushi-style) into 5 or 6 slices.

7. Slightly overlap the slices on warmed plates, pour the sauce over the top, and garnish with parsley. Serve immediately.

chicken breasts Marsala

Serves: 4
Cooking time: 1 to 4 hours

1. Fill and preheat the water oven to 146°F (63.5°C).

2. Drizzle the chicken with a tablespoon of the olive oil and season with salt, pepper, and chopped thyme.

3. Divide the chicken between two small (1 quart/.9 liter) cooking pouches and vacuum seal.

4. Submerge the pouches in the water oven and cook for at least 1 hour and up to 4 hours.

5. Remove the chicken from the pouches and pat dry.

6. Heat the remaining olive oil in a skillet over medium-high heat.

7. Sear the chicken in the skillet to a nice golden brown, about 1 minute per side. Transfer the chicken to a plate and tent with foil.

8. In the same skillet, melt 2 tablespoons of the butter, add the mushrooms, and cook until they begin to brown, about 5 minutes. Add the garlic and cook for 1 to 2 more minutes, then sprinkle in the flour and cook, stirring, for a minute or two more.

9. Reduce the heat to medium, carefully add the Marsala and the chicken stock, and simmer for a minute or two, gently scraping the bottom to deglaze the pan and pick up the flavorful brown bits.

10. Stir in the mascarpone and Dijon and combine thoroughly.

11. Return the chicken to the skillet and simmer for about 10 minutes while the sauce reduces. Add the last tablespoon of butter at the end for additional silkiness.

12. To serve, arrange the chicken breasts on a warmed platter and spoon the sauce with the mushrooms over them. Sprinkle with grated Parmesan cheese and fresh parsley, and serve over pasta or wild rice.

4 boneless, skinless chicken breast halves

3 tablespoons (45 ml) olive oil, divided use

Salt and pepper to taste

2 sprigs fresh thyme, chopped

3 tablespoons (30 ml) butter

1 pound (16 oz/473 g) crimini, oyster or shitake mushrooms

2 cloves garlic, peeled and minced

2 tablespoons Wondra® Quick-Mix Flour (or regular white flour)

1 cup (8 oz/237 ml)) Marsala wine

3/4 cup (6 oz/177 ml) chicken stock

1/2 cup (4 oz/120 g) mascarpone cheese

2 tablespoons (30 ml) Dijon mustard

2 tablespoons (30 ml) freshly grated Parmesan cheese, for garnish

4 tablespoons (60 ml) chopped Italian parsley, for garnish

Cooked wild rice or pasta for serving

chicken curry with lentils and rice

Serves 4
Cooking time: 4 to 6 hours

1. Fill and preheat the water oven to 176°F (80°C).

2. Put the red lentils in a pan and add the curry powder, ground coriander, cumin seeds and stock.

3. Bring the mixture to a boil, lower the heat, and cover. Simmer gently, stirring often, until the lentils are soft and most of the liquid is absorbed, (about 30 minutes).

4. When the lentils are cooked, drain any excess liquid and set aside.

5. Sprinkle salt and freshly ground pepper on both sides of the chicken thighs.

6. Divide the chicken thighs, shredded spinach, and lentil mixture between two large (1 gallon/3.8 liter) zip-closure cooking pouches. Evacuate the air from the pouches (page 11) and seal.

7. Submerge the pouches in the water oven and cook for a minimum of 4 hours and up to 6 hours. The food must be submerged completely to ensure even cooking.

Prepare the rice

1. Put the rice and water into a small (1 quart/.9 liter) zip-closure cooking pouch. Evacuate the air from the pouch (page 11) and seal.

2. Submerge the pouch in the water oven 1 hour and 15 minutes before the chicken is done. Remove promptly after 1 hour and 15 minutes.

Assemble the meal

1. Remove the cooking pouches from the water oven, and let them rest for 5 minutes.

2. Fluff the rice with a fork, and spoon onto a serving platter.

3. Using a slotted spoon, remove the thighs from their pouches and place on the platter with the rice. Spoon the spinach and lentils over the chicken, adding the juices from the pouch as desired.

4. Garnish with fresh coriander, and serve.

For the curry

$2/3$ cup (9 oz/150g) red lentils, rinsed

4 tablespoons (60 ml) curry powder (hot or mild)

4 teaspoons (20 ml) ground coriander

2 teaspoon (10 ml) cumin seeds

2 cups (6 oz/475 ml) vegetable stock

8 skinless chicken thighs

8 oz (225 g) fresh spinach, shredded

Salt and freshly ground pepper

For the rice

1 cup (6.5 oz/192 g) white or brown Basmati rice, rinsed

2 cups (16 oz/473 ml) water

For the garnish

Fresh coriander, chopped

chicken kebabs

Serves 4
Cooking time: 1½ to 2 hours

1. In a bowl, mix the olive oil, lemon juice, garlic, and seasonings. Cover and refrigerate for 30 minutes before using.

2. Assemble the kebabs by alternating pieces of vegetables to fill 4 skewers and pieces of chicken to fill another 4 skewers.

3. Put the vegetable skewers into one large (1 gallon/3.8 liter) zip-closure bag and the chicken skewers into another one. Pour half the marinade over the vegetables and half over the chicken. Refrigerate for 4 hours.

Cook the kebabs

1. Fill and preheat the water oven to 183°F (84°C).

2. Remove the vegetable skewers from the marinade, and pat them lightly with a paper towel to remove the excess. Put them, separately, into appropriately-sized cooking pouches (depending on the length of the skewer), and vacuum seal. Repeat with the chicken skewers and refrigerate until ready to cook. Discard the remaining marinade.

3. Submerge the vegetable pouches in the water oven and cook for 30 minutes.

4. After 30 minutes, and with the vegetable pouches still in the water bath, drop the temperature of the water oven to 146°F (56.5°C), adding ice and cold water to hasten the drop.

5. Submerge the pouch of chicken skewers in the water oven to cook for 1 hour and up to 2 hours.

Finish and serve

1. Remove the kebabs from the water bath, and if desired, sear the exterior of the kebabs on a hot grill or grill pan, or with a kitchen torch.

2. Plate the kebabs with the cooked rice and serve.

For the marinade

¹/₄ cup (2 oz/60 ml) olive oil

¹/₂ cup (4 oz/120 ml) lemon juice

2 tablespoons (30 ml) grated onion

1 clove garlic, peeled and pressed

¹/₄ teaspoon (1.25 ml) coarse salt

¹/₄ teaspoon (1.25 ml) freshly ground black pepper

¹/₄ teaspoon (1.25 ml) paprika

1 tablespoon (15 ml) chopped fresh parsley or 1 teaspoon (5 ml) dried

For the kebab assembly

2 large red bell peppers, stemmed, cored, and cut into bite-size chunks

2 large green bell peppers, stemmed, cored, and cut into bite-size chunks

12 to 16 pearl onions, peeled

4 boneless, skinless chicken breast halves, cut into bite-size chunks

4 large metal or pre-soaked wooden skewers

For serving

2 cups (13.75 oz/390 g) cooked white or brown Basmati rice

chicken Afrique

Serves 6
Cooking time: 2 ½ to 4 hours

1. Fill and preheat the water oven to 146°F (63°C).

2. In a skillet over medium-high heat, melt the coconut oil and brown the chicken breasts in it. Transfer them to a plate to cool.

3. Reduce heat to medium and sauté the onions in the skillet until limp. Add the garlic, chile pepper, curry, oregano, salt and pepper, and continue to cook and stir for another minute.

4. In a small bowl, whisk the tomato paste into the chicken broth to blend and pour the mixture into the skillet. Add the bay leaf and bring all to a boil.

5. Return the chicken to the skillet and coat the breasts all over with the tomato sauce. Reserve any remaining sauce in the skillet.

6. Put three chicken breasts into each of two large (1 gallon/3.8 liter) cooking pouches and vacuum seal.

7. Submerge the pouches in the water oven and cook for 2 ½ hours, and up to 4 hours.

8. A few minutes before serving, return the skillet with tomato sauce to the burner over medium heat, add the olive oil and the chopped bell pepper, and cook until the pepper has softened.

9. Add the peanut butter and sherry (or vinegar) to the skillet, and stir to combine.

10. Remove the chicken from the water oven, open the pouch and drain the accumulated liquid into the saucepan with the peanut sauce. Mix well.

11. Transfer the chicken to a warm serving platter, pour the combined sauce over the chicken, and serve with rice.

1 tablespoon (15 ml) coconut oil

6 boneless, skinless chicken breast halves, washed and patted dry

2 onions, peeled and chopped

4 cloves garlic, peeled and minced

1 long red or green chile pepper, seeded and minced

2 teaspoons (10 ml) curry powder

¼ teaspoon dried oregano

1 teaspoon (5 ml) sea salt

½ teaspoon (2.5 ml) coarsely ground black pepper

½ cup (4 oz/118 ml) chicken broth

1 small can (6 oz/170 g) tomato paste

1 bay leaf

1 teaspoon (5 ml) olive oil

1 red bell pepper, stemmed, cored, and finely chopped

½ cup (4.4 oz/129 g) peanut butter

2 tablespoons (30 ml) sherry or white balsamic vinegar

3 cups cooked white rice for serving

fried chicken and mashed potatoes

Courtesy of Vivian Peterson

Serves 4
Cooking time: 4 hours

Cook the potatoes

1. Fill and preheat the water oven to 180-185°F (82-85°C).

2. Put the potatoes into cooking pouches, evenly distributed in a single layer without overcrowding, and vacuum seal.

3. Submerge the pouch(es) in the water oven to cook for 1½ hours, until quite tender.

4. Meanwhile, in a skillet on the stove top, melt the butter and sauté the garlic and parsley until very slightly brown.

5. Remove the potato pouches from the water oven, open them, and drain the accumulated liquid away.

6. Put the potatoes into a food processor work bowl or a blender, add the sautéed garlic and parsley, the cream, and the truffle salt, and purée until smooth.

7. Put the mashed potatoes into a large (1 gallon/3.8 liter) zip-closure cooking pouch, evacuate the air (page 11), and seal. Put the pouch in the water oven.

Cook the chicken

1. Reset the temperature in the water bath to 140°F (60°C). To speed the process along, remove 1 to 2 quarts/liters of hot water from the water bath with a large measuring cup and replace it with an equivalent amount of ice water.

2. Sprinkle chicken all over with sumac powder and smoked black pepper.

3. Arrange the pieces in a single layer in a large (1 gallon/3.8 liter) cooking pouch and vacuum seal.

4. Submerge the pouch in the water oven and cook for 2½ hours.

For the potatoes

5 to 6 russet potatoes, peeled and diced

4 tablespoons (57 g) butter

⅓ cup (12 g) fresh flat leaf Italian parsley chopped

2 tablespoons (30 ml) chopped fresh garlic

½ cup (120 ml) heavy whipping cream

1 to 2 teaspoons (5 to 10 ml) truffle salt, to taste

For the chicken

8 chicken thighs

3 tablespoons (45 ml) sumac powder

3 tablespoons (45 ml) smoked black pepper

For the strawberry corn relish

1 teaspoon (5 ml) smoked sea salt

4 spring onions (scallions), trimmed and chopped

2 cups (16 oz/450 g) corn kernels

1 tablespoon (15 ml) champagne vinegar

1 tablespoon (15 g) butter

6 ripe strawberries, trimmed and chopped

For the chicken coating

2 cups (198 g) all-purpose flour

3 eggs

2 cups (198 g) panko bread crumbs

1 cup (180 g) Parmesan cheese

1 teaspoon (5 ml) salt or to taste

4 tablespoons (60 ml) Mediterranean herb seasoning

2 teaspoons (10 ml) chili (red pepper) flakes

1 quart (0.9 liter) vegetable oil

Prepare the strawberry corn relish

1. In a cast iron pan, over medium high heat, add the smoked sea salt, then the scallions, and lightly sauté until the scallions are softened.

2. Add the corn and continue to cook for 1 minute.

3. Stir in the vinegar and transfer the mixture to a bowl.

4. Add the butter and stir lightly.

5. Fold in the fresh strawberries and set aside until time to serve.

Prepare the chicken coating mixture in 3 wide, shallow bowls

1. Put the flour in the first bowl.

2. Whisk the eggs in the second.

3. Fill the third bowl with a mixture of the panko bread crumbs, Parmesan cheese, salt, herb seasoning, and chili flakes.

Finish the chicken

1. Remove the chicken from the water oven, open the pouches, and one-by-one, dredge each thigh first in flour, then dip in the egg wash, and then roll in the panko mixture until fully covered.

2. Heat the vegetable oil in a skillet on the stove top.

3. Working in batches, drop the chicken pieces gently, one by one, into the hot oil, turning all sides until fried crispy. Do not overcrowd the pan.

4. Remove cooked chicken to a paper-towel-lined plate to drain.

Plate and serve

1. Remove the mashed potato pouch from the water bath, and put a scoop on each plate.

2. Add the chicken thighs and strawberry corn relish, and serve.

braised turkey legs

Courtesy of Pam McKinstry

Serves 8
Cooking time: 8 to 12 hours

1. In a small bowl, thoroughly combine the tomato paste and chicken stock and pour in ½ cup (4 oz/118 ml) portions into four zip-closure cooking pouches, and freeze several hours or overnight.

2. Fill and preheat the water oven to 175°F (79°C).

3. Remove the skin from the turkey legs, along with any silver skin or tough membranes. (The skin can also be removed after the legs are cooked, or left on and seared before serving, if desired.)

4. Season the poultry with salt and pepper, then rub 1 tablespoon (15 ml) garlic confit over each leg.

5. Put one leg in a large (1 gallon/3.8 liter) cooking pouch, and add ½ tablespoon (2.5ml) of the thyme leaves, 1 bay leaf, 2 strips of the orange zest, 1 sprig of the rosemary, and 1 portion of the frozen tomato paste and chicken stock mixture. Repeat with the remaining legs, and vacuum seal the pouches.

6. Submerge the pouches in the water oven and cook for at least 8 hours, and up to 12 hours.

7. Open the pouches, drain the accumulated liquid into a container, and set the turkey legs aside.

8. If serving with the skin on, preheat the broiler to high and brown the turkey legs under the broiler.

9. Strain the liquid from the pouches through a fine mesh sieve into a large skillet, and discard the solids.

10. Bring the liquid to a boil over medium-high heat, add the white wine, and continue to boil until the sauce is reduced to about 1½ cups (12 oz/355 ml).

11. Add the turkey legs and cooked vegetables, if using, to the sauce, and reheat, covered, over low heat. Just before serving, stir the butter into the sauce.

12. Divide the legs and vegetables among four warm shallow bowls, and ladle some of the sauce over each portion.

13. Garnish with minced parsley and serve hot.

4 teaspoons (20 ml) tomato paste

2 cups (16 oz/473 ml) chicken stock

4 fresh turkey legs, each leg about 2½ inches (6.5 cm) thick

Kosher salt and freshly ground black pepper to taste

4 tablespoons (60 ml) mashed garlic confit

1½ teaspoons (7.5 ml) fresh thyme leaves

4 bay leaves

8 strips orange zest

4 small sprigs fresh rosemary

2 tablespoons (30 ml) white wine

1 tablespoon (15 ml) butter

For serving

Cooked root vegetables, such as carrots and parsnips

Minced fresh parsley

stuffed turkey enchilada

Courtesy of Sally MacColl

Serves 6 to 8
Cooking time: 5 to 7 hours

Cook the turkey tenders

1. Fill and preheat the water oven to 146°F (63°C).

2. Wash and completely dry the tenders and sprinkle with salt and pepper.

3. Put one tender per pouch into two small (1 quart/.9 liter) cooking pouches, add half the butter or fat to each pouch, and vacuum seal.

4. Submerge the pouches in the water oven and cook for 4 hours, and up to 6 hours.

5. Remove the turkey from the pouches and set aside.

Assemble the enchilada

1. Preheat a conventional oven to 375°F (190°C).

2. Cut the turkey into $\frac{1}{2}$-inch (1.3 cm) pieces.

3. Put a thin layer of enchilada sauce on the bottom of an 8 x 8-inch (20 x 20-cm) casserole.

4. In a medium bowl combine the remaining enchilada sauce, sour cream, and ground cumin, and stir until thoroughly blended.

5. Cut 2 to 3 tortillas to fit the casserole dish, and arrange them on top of the enchilada sauce. (It doesn't have to be perfect; it's basically like lasagna.) Sprinkle this first layer of tortillas with about a third of the turkey, cheese, and green chiles. Pour about a third of the sauce mixture on top.

6. Cut another layer of tortillas and repeat with another third of the turkey, cheese, and chiles. Top with another third of the sauce mixture.

7. Repeat for the final layer, using all of the remaining tortillas, turkey, cheese, and chiles, and cilantro, if desired. Pour the remaining sauce on top.

8. Bake for about 40 minutes or until the casserole is bubbling and beginning to brown around the edges. Top with the reserved cheese and cook for another 5 minutes or until the cheese has turned a golden brown.

9. Remove from the oven and allow to rest before cutting into individual servings. The results are even better if the enchilada is allowed to cool, refrigerated up to overnight, and reheated in a conventional oven at 350°F (177°C) for about 20 to 30 minutes before serving.

2 whole turkey tenders

Kosher or sea salt

Freshly ground black pepper

3 tablespoons (45 ml) unsalted butter, duck fat, or lard

1 can (28 oz/828 ml) canned green enchilada sauce

2 cups (16 oz/454 g) sour cream

1 tablespoon (15 ml) ground cumin

10 to 12 fresh corn tortillas

$2\frac{1}{2}$ cups (10 oz/296 g) jalapeño jack cheese, coarsely grated, reserving about $\frac{1}{2}$ cup (2.2 oz/65 g) for final browning

1 can (4 oz/113 g) roasted green chiles, mild or hot, chopped

Chopped cilantro

meatball soup with rainbow chard

Serves 6
Cooking time: 2 to 4 hours

Prepare the meatballs

1. In a bowl, mix the egg, bread crumbs, Parmesan cheese, poultry seasoning, salt and pepper. Add the turkey and knead to combine thoroughly.

2. Form the mixture into 1-inch (2.5 cm) balls and refrigerate for one hour.

Make the soup

1. Fill and preheat the water oven to 183°F (84°C).

2. Season the chicken broth with the sea salt, black pepper, garlic powder, onion powder, and cayenne pepper. Divide the broth between two large (1 gallon/3.8 liter) zip-closure cooking pouches.

3. Add the onion and meatballs to the cooking pouches, evacuate the air (page 11), and seal.

4. Put the carrots and chard into two small (1 quart/.9 liter) cooking pouches and vacuum seal.

5. Submerge the pouches in the water oven and cook for at least 2 hours and up to 4 hours. The food must be completely submerged to ensure even cooking.

6. When ready, remove the pouches and put the carrots and chard into soup bowls. Ladle the broth mixture and meatballs into the bowls, and serve. Garnish with fresh grated Parmesan cheese.

For the meatballs

1 large egg, beaten

$^1/_4$ cup (1 oz/28 g) bread crumbs

$^1/_4$ cup (0.9 oz/25 g) grated Parmesan cheese, plus some for serving

$^3/_4$ teaspoon (3.75 ml) poultry seasoning

$^3/_4$ teaspoon (3.75 ml) salt

$^1/_4$ teaspoon (1.25 ml) ground black pepper

$^3/_4$ pound (12 0z/.34 kg) ground turkey

For the broth

6 cups (48 oz/1.4 liters) chicken broth

1 teaspoon (5 ml) sea salt

$^1/_2$ teaspoon (2.5 ml) ground black pepper

$^1/_4$ teaspoon (1.25 ml) garlic powder

$^1/_4$ teaspoon (1.25 ml) onion powder

Dash of cayenne pepper

For the vegetables

2 large carrots, peeled and cut into $^1/_4$-inch (1.25-cm) coins

1 large bunch (8 oz/240 g) rainbow chard, trimmed and chopped

1 small onion, peeled, halved, and sliced

turkey tenderloin and tomato chutney

Courtesy of Chef Richard Blais

Serves 4
Cooking time: 4 to 6 hours

1. Fill and preheat the water oven to 185°F (85°C).

2. Combine all the chutney ingredients in a zip-closure cooking pouch. Evacuate the air from the pouch (page 11) and seal.

3. Submerge the pouch in the water oven and cook for a minimum of 30 minutes and up to 1 hour. The food must be submerged completely to ensure even cooking.

4. Quick chill the chutney by submerging the pouch in an ice water bath (half ice, half water) for at least 30 minutes, and then refrigerate in the pouch until ready to use, or up to several days.

Cook the turkey

1. Fill and preheat the water oven to 146°F (63°C).

2. Sprinkle the tenderloins with salt and pepper.

3. Vacuum seal each tenderloin in a small (1 quart/.9 liter) cooking pouch.

4. Submerge the pouches in the water oven and cook for at least 4 hours and up to 6 hours.

5. If serving the tomato chutney warm, add the chilled pouches to the water oven with the turkey for the last hour of cooking.

6. When ready, remove the turkey tenderloins to a serving platter, and serve with the tomato chutney.

For the tomato chutney

1 can (14.5 ounces/411g) diced tomatoes, drained

$^1/_2$ teaspoon (2.5 ml) ground ginger

$^1/_2$ teaspoon (2.5 ml) garlic powder

$^1/_4$ teaspoon (1.25 ml) ground cumin

$^1/_2$ teaspoon (2.5 ml) ground coriander

2 whole cloves

2 teaspoons (10 ml) mustard seed

$^1/_4$ teaspoon (1.25 ml) cayenne pepper

$^1/_2$ cup (4.25 oz/120 g) diced onion

1 teaspoon (5 ml) ghee (clarified butter) or unsalted butter

For the turkey

4 turkey tenderloins

1 teaspoon (5 ml) salt

1 teaspoon (5 ml) pepper

nutty bird burgers with mango salsa

Serves 4
Cooking time: 45 to 90 minutes

1. In a bowl, add all cheeseburger ingredients and mix well with clean hands to thoroughly combine the flavors.

2. Form into patties and put them into the freezer for a couple of hours to firm them.

Cook the burgers

1. Fill and preheat the water oven to 160°F (71°C).

2. Put the patties into a large (1 gallon/3.8 liter) cooking pouch in a single layer and vacuum seal.

3. Submerge the pouch in the water oven and cook for at least 45 minutes and up to 90 minutes.

Make the mango salsa

1. In a bowl, combine the garlic, Serrano pepper, vinegar, salt and pepper, and let the mixture sit for 10 to 15 minutes.

2. Whisk in the olive oil to emulsify.

3. Add the remaining ingredients and toss to coat.

4. Serve immediately or chill, if desired, for serving later.

Finish the cheeseburgers

1. Remove the patties from the pouch, pat them dry with a paper towel, brush with a bit of olive oil, and sear on a hot grill for color.

2. Dress with the mango salsa or your favorite condiments, and serve.

For the cheeseburgers

1 pound (16 oz/454 g) ground turkey

2 tablespoons (30 ml) fresh flat leaf parsley, minced

1 tablespoon (15 ml) fresh chives, minced

$1/2$ cup (2 oz/56.5 g) pepper jack (or cheddar) cheese shreds

$1/4$ cup (1 oz/30 g) pine nuts

1 tablespoon (15 ml) extra virgin olive oil

$1/2$ teaspoon (2.5 ml) garlic powder

$1/4$ teaspoon (1.2 ml) onion powder

$1/2$ teaspoon (2.5 ml) salt or to taste

$1/4$ teaspoon (1.2 ml) ground black pepper or to taste

For the mango salsa

2 cloves garlic, peeled and finely minced

1 Serrano pepper, seeded and minced

2 ounces (60 ml) white wine or champagne vinegar

Salt and pepper to taste

2 fluid ounces (60 ml) olive oil

4 fresh mangos, peeled and chopped

4 green onions, trimmed, white and green parts chopped

1 red pepper, cored and diced

1 red onion, peeled and diced

entrées

venison with juniper berry sauce

Courtesy of Douglas Baldwin, *Sous Vide for the Home Cook*
(Paradox Press, 2010)

Serves 8
Cooking time: 8 to 36 hours, depending on the cut

1. Fill and preheat the water oven to 130°F (55°C) for medium-rare; 140°F (60°C) for medium.

2. Lightly season the meat and vacuum seal each piece of venison in a separate cooking pouch and submerge the pouches in the water bath to cook. If the meat is from the rib or loin region, cook it for 6 to 8 hours; if it is from hip region, cook it for 12 to 18 hours; if it is from the shoulder or rump region, cook it for 24 to 36 hours.

3. Remove the venison from the pouches and pat dry with paper towels.

4. Heat the oil in a heavy skillet over high heat, watching carefully, until it just begins to smoke. Put two pieces of venison into the pan and sear all sides until deep brown. Remove to a platter and tent with foil to keep warm.

5. Wipe out the pan and repeat with the remaining venison.

6. Pour the excess oil out of the pan. Turn the heat down to medium, add the cognac, and scrape the brown bits off the bottom of the pan.

7. When the pan is almost dry, add the stock, juniper berries, current jelly and thyme and continue to cook, stirring frequently, until reduced by half.

8. Add the cream and cook until thickened.

9. Season with salt and pepper.

10. Pour the sauce over the venison and serve immediately.

2 pounds (32 oz/1 kg) venison, divided into four 8-ounce (225-g) pieces

2-3 tablespoons (30-40 ml) high smoke point oil (grapeseed, peanut, safflower)

Salt and black pepper to taste

For the juniper berry sauce

1/4 cup (60 ml) cognac

1 cup (250 ml) chicken stock

2 teaspoons (10 ml) dried juniper berries

1 tablespoon (15 ml) red currant jelly

1/4 teaspoon (1 ml) dried thyme

1/2 cup (125 ml) heavy cream

Salt and black pepper to taste

pulled wild pig

Courtesy of Rex Bird

Serves 20
Cooking time: 24 hours

1. Fill and preheat the water oven to 160°F (71°C).

2. Combine all brine ingredients in a large pot or jumbo heavy-duty zip-closure bag and stir until the salt is dissolved.

3. Cut the pork loins into 2-inch-thick (5-cm) slices, add to the brine solution, and cover or zip-seal. Refrigerate for 6 to 8 hours.

4. Remove the pork from brine, rinse under clear water, and pat dry.

5. In a small bowl, thoroughly combine all ingredients for the seasoning rub.

6. Baste the pork with olive oil, apply the seasoning rub, and divide the pork equally among cooking pouches, arranging the slices in a single layer.

7. Divide the bay leaves, thyme, and garlic among the pouches and vacuum seal.

8. Submerge the pouches in the water oven and cook for 24 hours.

9. When ready to serve, heat the barbecue sauce.

10. Remove the pork from pouches, pull the meat apart with fingers or forks, and mix thoroughly with barbecue sauce.

11. Serve piled on a toasted bun or on a plate with your favorite sides.

10 pounds (4.5 kg) wild pig pork loins

8 bay leaves

1 bunch fresh thyme

2 cloves garlic, smashed and peeled

4 teaspoons (20 ml) olive oil

For the brine

5 tablespoons (60ml) pickling spice

2 tablespoons (30 ml) whole black peppercorns

$\frac{1}{2}$ cup (96 g) cane sugar

1 cup (115 g) Kosher salt

1 gallon (3.8 liters) water

1 bunch fresh thyme leaves

For the seasoning rub

4 tablespoons (60 ml) smoked paprika

2 tablespoons (30 ml) coarsely ground black pepper

2 tablespoons (30 ml) chile powder

2 tablespoons (30 ml) brown sugar (optional)

1 tablespoon (15 ml) dry mustard

1 teaspoon (5 ml) ancho chile powder, or to taste

1 teaspoon (5 ml) cayenne powder, or to taste

For serving

Barbecue sauce (as you like it)

Toasted buns

Asian marinated boar foreshanks

Courtesy of Chef Heath Schecter

Serves 2
Cooking time: 36 hours

1. Fill and preheat the water oven to 165°F (74°C).

2. In a bowl, combine and whisk together all ingredients for the marinade.

3. Put the shanks into a large zip-closure bag, pour the marinade over, zip the seal, and refrigerate for 2 to 4 hours.

4. Remove the shanks from the marinade, put into individual cooking pouches, and vacuum seal. Discard marinade.

5. Submerge the pouches in the water oven and cook for 36 hours.

Make the pickled cucumbers

1. One hour before serving, put all ingredients into a zip-closure cooking pouch, evacuate the air (page 11), and vacuum seal.

2. Allow to marinate for one hour at room temperature.

Finish the boar shanks

1. Heat the broiler or a lightly oiled grill or skillet to high heat. Remove the shanks from the pouches, reserving accumulated liquid, and sear the surface until brown—about 5 minutes.

2. Pour the pouch liquid into a pan on the stove top and reduce over medium heat to create a light sauce.

3. Spoon a little of the sauce over the shanks, and serve with cooked rice and pickled cucumbers.

Serving variation: pulled pork tacos

1. Pull the meat off the shanks and put into soft corn tortillas.

2. Serve with homemade pickled cucumbers or slaw.

2 wild boar shanks

For the marinade

1 knob fresh ginger, peeled and sliced julienne

2 tablespoons (28 g) garlic, minced

1 cup (8 oz/240 ml) light soy sauce

1$\frac{1}{2}$ tablespoons (22.5 ml) mirin

2 tablespoons (30 ml) sriracha

3 tablespoons (45 ml) rice wine vinegar

1 tablespoon (15 ml) Chinese 5 spice powder

$\frac{1}{2}$ cup (4 oz/120 ml) ketchup

$\frac{1}{4}$ cup (0.4oz/12.5 g) fresh chives, chopped

$\frac{1}{4}$ cup (2 oz/60 ml) olive oil

For the pickled cucumbers:

1 English cucumber, sliced

$\frac{1}{2}$ cup (4 oz/120 ml) rice vinegar

$\frac{1}{2}$ teaspoon (2.5 ml) salt

$\frac{1}{2}$ teaspoon (2.5 ml) sugar

1 Thai chili, minced

For serving:

1 cup (6 oz/170 g) basmati rice, cooked

Corn tortillas for serving variation

fennel-scented Cornish game hens

2 Cornish game hens, about 1½ to 2 pounds (24 oz/709 g to 32 oz/946 g) each

4 large cloves garlic confit

1 generous teaspoon (5 ml) finely minced preserved lemon

2 tablespoons (30 ml) fennel pollen

Kosher or sea salt and freshly ground black pepper to taste

2 tablespoons (60 ml) unsalted butter, cut in half

Olive oil

Courtesy of Pam McKinstry

Serves 2 to 4
Cooking time: 5 to 8 hours

Spatchcock the hens

1. Thoroughly wash the hens in cold water, pat them dry, and position them, breast side down, on a stable cutting surface.

2. Using poultry shears, insert one blade into the hen at the cavity just beside the backbone, cut up one side of the backbone, then down the other, and remove it. Repeat with other hen.

3. Spread the cavities apart and seek out the diamond-shaped breast bones. Carefully use the tip of a sharp paring knife to cut around the edges of each breast bone all the way around, without cutting into the meat. Loosen each bone and lift it from the cavity, snipping attachment points as needed with the shears, and remove it.

4. Splay the legs to flatten the spatchcocked birds and set them on a large plate, cutting board, or a piece of wax paper.

Cook the hens

1. Fill and preheat water oven to 155°F (68°C).

2. Mash the garlic confit with the preserved lemon to make a paste.

3. Spread half of the paste on one of the birds, rubbing it on both the skin side and the cavity side. Repeat with the second hen.

4. Sprinkle half of the fennel pollen on both sides of one of the birds and liberally season with salt and pepper. Repeat with the second hen.

7. Put each hen into its own large (1 gallon/3.8 liter) cooking pouch and vacuum seal.

9. Submerge the pouches in the water oven and cook the hens for at least 5 hours and up to 8 hours.

10. Remove the pouches from the water oven and open them immediately, being careful to retain all of the cooking juices. Set the hens aside and let them rest for 10 to 15 minutes.

Make the sauce

1. In a small saucepan over medium heat, cook the accumulated juices from the cooking pouches until they are reduced by half.

2. Keep the sauce warm while you finish the hens on the grill or stove top.

fennel-scented
Cornish game hens

continued from page 131

To finish the hens on the grill:

1. Heat a barbecue grill on high. Make sure the grate is very clean, to keep the delicate skin from sticking.

2. Drizzle the skin side of the hens with a little bit of olive oil and put them, skin side down, on the grill. Cook until the skin is crisp and golden, about 3 to 4 minutes. If desired, turn the birds over and cook another minute.

To finish the hens on the stove top:

1. Heat a ridged cast-iron pan over high heat until very hot.

2. Drizzle the hens with a little olive oil and put them, skin side down, in the pan. Cook until the skin is crisp and golden, about 3 to 4 minutes. If desired, turn the birds over and cook another minute.

Assemble the meal

1. Just before serving, whisk one piece of the butter into the warm sauce. When it has melted, whisk in the remaining piece.

2. Arrange the hens on a serving platter. Pour the reduced sauce over and serve.

Malabar duck

Courtesy of Chef Sam Hussain

Serves 2
Cooking time: 2½ hours

1. Remove the layer of fat from the duck breasts and score the meat.

2. In a bowl, combine 1 teaspoon (5 ml) of the ginger garlic paste with the salt and turmeric powder. Coat the breasts with the mixture, cover, and refrigerate for 30 minutes.

3. Meanwhile, fill and preheat the water oven to 140°F (60°C).

4. Put the marinated duck breasts into a cooking pouch and vacuum seal.

5. Submerge the pouch in the water oven to cook for 2½ hours.

Prepare the sauce spices

1. About 15 minutes before the cooking time expires, on the stove top, heat coconut oil in a thick-bottomed pan over medium heat and sauté the sliced shallots and curry leaves until golden brown.

2. Add the remaining ginger garlic paste, cashew nut, raisins and the all the remaining ground spices and cook for a minute more.

Finish the duck breasts

1. Remove the duck breasts from the cooking pouch, pat dry, add to the spice pan, and sear the surface well.

2. Remove the duck breasts and tent with foil to keep warm.

3. Add the tomato sauce and a little water to the pan, and simmer to your desired sauce thickness.

4. Finish by stirring in the coconut milk and salt.

Plate and serve

1. Put a pool of sauce on a warm plate.

2. Place a duck breast in the sauce, and garnish with carmelized onions.

2 duck breasts

4 teaspoons (20 ml) ginger garlic paste, divided use

Salt, to taste

1 teaspoon (5 ml) turmeric

For the sauce

1 teaspoon (5 ml) coconut oil

6 ounces (200 g) shallots, peeled

2 stems curry leaves

4 halves cashew nut

12 raisins

2 teaspoons (10 ml) Kashmiri chili powder

2 teaspoons (10 ml) ground coriander powder

½ teaspoon (2.5 ml) garam masala

1 can (14.5 oz/450 ml) tomato sauce

3½ ounces (100 ml) coconut milk

Salt, to taste

For plating

Caramelized onions

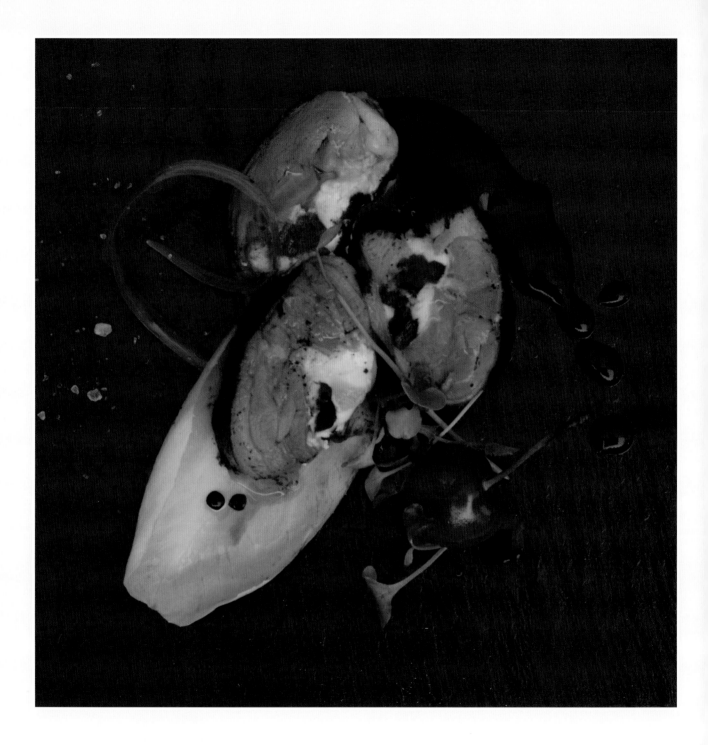

stuffed pheasant or duck breast

Serves 2
Cooking time: 2 to 4 hours

1. Fill and preheat the water oven to 135°F (57°C).

2. Macerate the dried cherries in the champagne for 10 minutes.

3. With a sharp knife, carefully cut a pocket into the side of the breasts lengthwise being careful not to cut all the way through the meat.

4. In a small mixing bowl, mix together the goat cheese, macerated cherries, and walnuts until well combined.

5. Stuff each breast with the mixture, season to taste with salt and pepper, and seal with a toothpick or kitchen twine.

6. Put the breasts into a small (1 quart/0.9 liter) cooking pouch and vacuum seal.

7. Submerge in the water oven and cook at least 2 hours, and up to 4 hours.

Make the sauce

1. About 15 minutes before the duck is ready to serve, in a saucepan over medium heat, melt 1 tablespoon (15 ml) of the butter into the olive oil, add the shallots, and sauté until translucent.

2. Add the port wine, orange juice, orange zest and cherries, and bring to a boil.

3. Simmer until the sauce reduces and thickens, mashing the cherries with the back of a wooden spoon to extract flavor as they cook, about 5 to 10 minutes. Taste and adjust seasonings with salt and pepper and the last moment, stir in the remaining butter to add silkiness to the sauce.

Finish the fowl

1. Preheat a skillet over high heat on the stove top.

2. Remove breasts from pouch, pat the skin dry with paper towels, and sear, skin side down in the hot skillet until the skin is golden and crispy.

3. Slice the breasts into ¼ inch (.6 cm) slices on a diagonal, arrange on serving plates, and pour the cherry port sauce over the top.

⅓ cup (1.8 oz/50 g) chopped dried cherries

1 cup (8 oz/240 ml) champagne

2 pheasant or duck breasts

½ cup (4.2 oz/120 g) goat cheese

¼ cup (1 oz/29 g) diced toasted walnuts

Salt and freshly ground black pepper

For the cherry port sauce

2 tablespoons (30 ml) butter, divided use

1 tablespoon (15 ml) pheasant/duck fat or olive oil

1 large or 2 small shallots, peeled and minced

¼ cup (2 oz/30 ml) ruby port wine

⅓ cup (2.8 oz/80 ml) freshly squeezed orange juice

1 teaspoon (5 ml) grated orange zest

½ cup (2.5 oz/70 g) pitted frozen black cherries, thawed and roughly chopped

duck breast with soubise sauce

Courtesy of Chef Jason Wilson

Serves 4
Cooking time: 2¼ hours for the soubise sauce
plus 45 minutes for the duck breasts

1. Fill and preheat the water oven to 180°F (82°C).

2. Put all soubise sauce ingredients into a small (1 quart/0.9 liter) zip-closure cooking pouch, evacuate the air (page 11), and seal.

3. Submerge the pouch in the water bath and cook for 2 hours. If not serving right away, quick chill the pouch by submerging it in an ice water bath (half ice, half water) for 30 minutes, and refrigerate for up to 48 hours.

Cook the duck breasts

1. Reset the temperature in the water bath to 140°F (60°C). To speed the process along, remove 1 to 2 quarts/liters of hot water from the water bath with a large measuring cup and replace it with an equivalent amount of ice water.

2. In a small bowl, combine the seasonings and spices, mixing well.

3. Season the duck with the spice mixture. Put 2 breasts in a single layer into each of 2 small (1 quart/0.9 liter) cooking pouches and vacuum seal.

4. Submerge the pouches in the water bath and cook for 20 to 30 minutes.

Finish the duck breasts and soubise sauce

1. Pour the contents of the soubise sauce pouch into a blender, and purée until smooth.

2. Slowly simmer in a pot and keep warm for service.

3. Remove the duck breasts from the pouches and allow 5 minutes for the meat to rest.

4. In a sauté pan over medium heat, slowly sear the breasts, fat side down, until fat is rendered and skin is crisp.

5. Spoon a fourth of the soubise sauce onto each serving plate. Place a duck breast on top of the sauce and garnish with huckleberries and figs.

For the soubise sauce

1 yellow onion, peeled and rough chopped

1 shallot, peeled and rough chopped

1 strip bacon, diced small

½ green apple, peeled and acidulated

½ cup (4 oz/120 ml) heavy cream

1 bay leaf

1 stalk celery, trimmed and rough chopped

1 whole clove

2 sprigs thyme

2 tablespoons (30 ml) kosher salt

For the duck breasts

2 tablespoons (30 ml) sassafras powder

1½ tablespoons (45 ml) kosher salt

4 sprigs fresh thyme, stripped for leaves

½ teaspoon (2.5 ml) ground black cardamom

4 Moulard duck breasts, trimmed of silver skin and excess fat

For plating

½ cup (2.4 oz/68 g) huckleberries

8 figs

duck confit

Courtesy of Pam McKinstry

Serves 4
Cooking time: 7 to 8 hours

Brine the duck legs

1. Wash the duck legs in cold water, pat them dry, and arrange them in a shallow baking dish that will hold them comfortably in a single layer.

2. In a small coffee grinder or spice mill, grind the cinnamon stick, star anise, and peppercorns into a fine powder. Transfer the spice mixture to a small bowl and add the garlic, orange zest, ginger, and salt. Stir to blend.

3. Sprinkle the salt-spice mixture (dry brine) over the duck legs, rubbing it on all surfaces of the flesh and skin. Cover the dish with plastic wrap and refrigerate the duck for 2 to 4 hours.

Cook the confit

1. Fill and preheat water oven to 180°F (82°C).

2. Rinse the duck legs thoroughly to remove the dry brine, put them in a bowl and cover them with cold water. Let sit for 5 minutes, then drain and repeat this process.

3. Dry the duck legs thoroughly with paper towels.

4. Put two duck legs into a small (1 quart/.9 liter) cooking pouch and add 1 cup of the duck fat to the pouch. Repeat with the remaining two legs and duck fat. Vacuum seal both pouches and refrigerate until you are ready to cook the duck.

5. Submerge the pouches and cook the legs for 7 hours if they are small (less than 8 oz/237 g each), or 8 hours if they are large.

6. Remove the pouches from the water bath and carefully open and remove the duck legs.

7. Drain off the liquid fat from the pouches, and refrigerate or freeze it for future use.

8. Just before serving, sear the duck legs in a hot skillet for 30 seconds to 1 minute per side, or put under a hot broiler for 3 to 5 minutes to crisp the skin.

4 Peking or Muscovy duck legs, skin on

1 (3-inch/7.6-cm) cinnamon stick, halved

2 star anise

$1/2$ teaspoon (2.5 ml) Szechuan peppercorns

2 large cloves garlic, peeled and smashed

1 orange, grated zest only

$1/2$ tablespoon (7.5 ml) fresh ginger, peeled and finely grated

$1/2$ cup (3.75 oz/110 g) coarse kosher salt

2 cups (16 oz/473 g) duck fat, cold

stuffed quail with goat cheese grits

Serves 4
Cooking time: 2 to 3 hours

Fill and preheat the water oven to 154°F (68°C).

Make the veal demi-glace

1. In a medium saucepan, combine the beef broth, carrots, garlic, and parsley. Simmer uncovered for about 1 hour and 15 minutes. Be sure to stir a few times while the sauce simmers. (Meanwhile make the stuffing and move on with the quail.)

2. After the simmering is complete the mixture will be greatly reduced. Now add the wine and continue to simmer 20 more minutes.

3. Whisk in the butter; once it is incorporated the demi-glace is ready.

Make the stuffing

1. In a medium skillet, over medium heat, melt 2 tablespoons (30 ml) of the butter with 1 tablespoon (15 ml) of the olive oil.

2. When the oil and butter are hot, add the onions, carrots, and celery, season to taste with salt and pepper, and sauté for 5 minutes. Add the garlic and cook for 1 to 2 more minutes. Transfer to a bowl and set aside.

3. In same skillet, add the remaining oil and butter over medium heat and sauté the mushrooms until soft, about 5 to 7 minutes.

4. Transfer the mushrooms to the bowl containing the vegetable mixture and combine to make the stuffing for the quail.

Stuff and cook the quail

1. Using a sharp knife or poultry shears, split each quail down the middle into two halves.

2. Season each quail half with salt, pepper and about ½ teaspoon (2.5 ml) of the Cajun seasoning.

3. Divide the stuffing into fourths and form the mixture into round balls.

4. With the quail skin side down, insert a ball of stuffing into the cavity of four of the quail halves.

For the veal demi-glace

2 cans (14 oz/414 ml each) low sodium beef broth

2 large carrots, peeled and cut into four pieces

4 cloves garlic, peeled and cut in half

½ cup (1.35 oz/39 g) fresh Italian parsley

½ cup (4 oz/118 ml) red wine (such as merlot)

6 tablespoons (90 ml) butter, cut into 6 pats

For the stuffing

4 tablespoons (60 ml) butter

2 tablespoons (30 ml) olive oil

1 cup (8.5 oz/251 g) chopped onions

½ cup (1 oz/30 g) chopped carrots

½ cup (1 oz/30 g) chopped celery

Salt and freshly ground black pepper to taste

2 cloves garlic, peeled and crushed

2 cups (6 oz/177 g) shitake mushrooms, chopped

For the quail

4 whole quail, semi-boneless

Salt and pepper to taste

4 teaspoons (20 ml) Cajun seasoning

For the goat cheese grits

4½ cups (36 oz/1 liter) milk

¼ cup (2 oz/60 ml) melted butter

Salt and pepper to taste

2 cups (11.5 oz/340 g) quick white grits

1½ cups (6 oz/170 g) goat cheese, crumbled

For the Madeira sauce

1 cup (8 oz/237 ml) Madeira

2 cups (16 oz/473 ml) prepared veal demi-glace

5. Put a stuffed quail half and an unstuffed half side-by-side in a small (1 quart/.9 liter) cooking pouch Repeat with the remaining quail halves, pairing stuffed with unstuffed.

6. Vacuum seal the pouches, submerge them in the water oven, and cook for at least 1 hour, and up to 3 hours.

Prepare the grits

1. In a saucepan, over medium heat, combine the milk and butter, and season with salt and pepper.

2. Bring the liquid to a boil and whisk in the grits, stirring constantly for 6 minutes or until tender.

3. Remove the pan from the heat and stir in the cheese. Taste and adjust seasonings. Cover and keep warm until ready to serve.

Finish the quail

1. When the quail have finished cooking, preheat the broiler of the conventional oven to high.

2. Remove the quail from the pouches, being careful not to lose the stuffing from the stuffed halves, and put them back together, securing them with kitchen twine.

3. Put the quail breast side up onto a broiler pan, and pat their surfaces dry with a paper towel.

4. Melt the remaining butter and brush the surface of the quail with it.

5. Brown the skin of the quail for 5 or 6 minutes under the broiler. Remove from the heat and tent with foil to keep warm.

Make the Madeira sauce

1. In a saucepan, over medium heat, bring the Madeira to a boil, and reduce the volume by half—about 4 minutes.

2. Whisk in the veal demi-glace and simmer for another 2 to 3 minutes.

Plate the meal

1. Spoon a portion of the grits onto the center of each plate.

2. Place one quail on top of the grits, and remove the twine.

3. Spoon the Madeira sauce over the quail.

rabbit loin

Courtesy of Chef Heath Schecter

Serves 4
Cooking time: 4 hours

1. Fill and preheat the water oven to 150°F (65.5°C).

2. In a bowl, mix all ingredients for the marinade and put the loins in the mixture, making sure to coat them well all over.

3. Put each loin into a small (1 quart/0.9 liter) cooking pouch and vacuum seal.

4. Submerge the sealed pouches in the water oven to cook for 4 hours.

5. To finish, heat the oil in a skillet until hot.

6. Remove the loins from their pouches, pat dry, and sear the loins on both sides.

7. Plate with side dishes as desired.

4 (8-ounce/228-g) rabbit loins

2 tablespoons (30ml) olive oil or high-smoke point vegetable oil

For the marinade

2 tablespoons (30 ml) chopped fresh flat leaf parsley

1 tablespoon (15 ml) chopped fresh dill

2 tablespoons (30 ml) Dijon mustard

1 teaspoon (5 ml) apple cider vinegar

$\frac{1}{4}$ cup (2 oz/60 ml) olive oil

1 teaspoon (5 ml) minced garlic

$\frac{1}{2}$ teaspoon (2.5 ml) freshly ground black pepper

$\frac{1}{4}$ teaspoon (1.25 ml) ground ginger

1 healthy pinch kosher salt

prosciutto-wrapped rabbit saddle

Courtesy of Chef Jason Wilson

Serves 4
Cooking time: 4 hours

1. Fill and preheat the water oven to 164°F (73.5°C).

2. Grind the bacon, pork butt, rabbit hind leg meat and herbs through the small die of a meat grinder.

3. Put the ground meat, cream, spices and brandy into the work bowl of a food processor and purée until smooth to make a rabbit mousse.

4. Pass the mousse through a fine tamis or sieve, so that the resulting mixture is free of sinew.

5. Chill the mousse for 30 minutes in the refrigerator.

6. Lay 3 of the slices of prosciutto onto of a sheet of cooking-safe plastic wrap (cling film) approximately 12 inches (30 cm) long, so that the prosciutto overlaps and provides a 6-inch (15-cm) wide sheet to work with.

7. Evenly cover the prosciutto with one-quarter of the mousse, spreading 1/3-inch (0.8-cm) thick, using a small offset spatula.

8. Place one rabbit loin in the center of the mousse and season lightly with kosher salt.

9. Slowly roll the prosciutto around the loin, so that the mousse and prosciutto encase it, pulling away the plastic wrap as you roll. Wrap the finished roll tightly in plastic wrap to create a compact cylinder. Repeat with the remaining rabbit loins.

10. Put the cylinders into cooking pouches and vacuum seal. Submerge in the water oven to cook for 4 hours.

11. Remove from the water oven and arrest the cooking by submerging the pouches in an ice-water bath, then remove the rabbit rolls from the vacuum pouches and plastic wrap, and pat dry.

12. On the stove top, heat a sauté pan to high heat and sear the cylinders on all sides.

13. Finish the roasting in a traditional oven, preheated to 350°F (177°C), for 6 minutes.

14. Meanwhile, in a skillet over medium-high heat, warm the olive oil, sauté the mushrooms and kale until tender, and warm the demi-glace. Season to taste with salt and pepper.

15. Slice and serve the rabbit with a drizzle of demi-glace and the sautéed mushrooms and kale.

1 pound (16 oz/0.45 kg) rabbit hind leg meat, boned, and diced large

1/4 pound (4 oz/114 g) bacon, diced large

1/4 pound (4 oz/114 g) pork butt, diced large

1/2 teaspoon (2.5 ml) each coriander, clove, fennel, and juniper berry, finely ground

1/2 cup (4 oz/120 ml) heavy cream

1 teaspoon (5 ml) fresh marjoram, finely chopped

1 teaspoon (5 ml) fresh thyme, finely chopped

1/4 cup (2 oz/60 ml) brandy

12 slices prosciutto

4 rabbit loins

Kosher salt as needed

For plating

1 tablespoon (15 ml) olive oil

6 to 8 ounces (170 to 226 g) maitake or chanterelle mushrooms

1 bunch dino kale, chiffonade

4 ounces (114 g) demi-glace

Salt and pepper to taste

elk roast

Courtesy of Chef Heath Schecter

Serves 4
Cooking time: 8 to 24 hours

1. Fill and preheat the water oven to 134°F (56.5°C).

2. In a bowl, combine and whisk together all ingredients for the marinade.

3. Put the elk into a zip-closure bag, pour in the marinade, zip the seal, and refrigerate for at least 2 hours, up to overnight.

4. Remove the elk from the marinade, put it into a cooking pouch, and vacuum seal. Discard the marinade.

5. Submerge the pouch in the water oven and cook for at least 8 hours, and up to 24 hours.

6. When ready to serve, preheat a grill or grill pan to high heat.

7. Remove the elk from the pouch, reserving pouch juices. Pat the roast dry with paper towels, and sear on the hot grill to brown the surface and enhance the smokiness. Remove to a carving platter and tent with foil to keep warm.

8. In a saucepan, heat the olive oil and sauté the minced shallots and garlic. Deglaze the pan with the red wine, and then add the reserved cooking pouch juices. Cook until reduced to a sauce; fortify with veal base or demi-glace if needed.

9. Carve the roast and pour the sauce over the meat. Serve with thick slices of russet potatoes and baby kale.

1 bone-in elk chuck roast, approximately 2 pounds (32 oz/0.9 kg)

For the marinade

1 sprig fresh parsley, minced

1 sprig fresh thyme, minced

1 sprig fresh rosemary, minced

1 sprig fresh oregano, minced

1 teaspoon (5 ml) cocoa powder

$1/4$ cup (2 oz/60 ml) olive oil

2 cloves garlic, peeled and minced

$1/2$ teaspoon (2.5 ml) pepper, fresh ground

$1/2$ teaspoon (2.5 ml) paprika, smoked

1 healthy pinch Kosher salt

2 tablespoons (30 ml) full-bodied red wine

For the sauce

2 tablespoons (60 ml) olive oil

1 shallot, peeled and minced

1 clove garlic, peeled and minced

$1/2$ cup (4 oz/120 ml) red wine

Elk roast cooking pouch juices

For serving:

Russet potatoes, cooked

Baby kale, cooked

entrées

sous vide salmon video

Scan the code with your smart phone,
or visit sousvidesupreme.com/thecookbook

lobster tail with vegetable salad

Courtesy of Chef Josh Horrigan

Serves 2
Cooking time: 1 hour

Cook the lobster

1. Fill and preheat the water oven to 138°F (59°C).

2. Put the lobster tails into a cooking pouch. Add the butter, yuzu juice, and fennel pollen.

3. Vacuum seal the pouch and submerge in the water bath to cook for 25 minutes.

4. Remove the pouch from the water oven and quick chill it in an ice water bath (half ice/half water) for 15 minutes, and then refrigerate.

Prepare the vegetables

1. Reset the temperature in the water bath to 170°F (77°C).

2. Peel the beets and put them in a single layer into cooking pouches, keeping the two types of beets in separate pouches to prevent the striped beats from bleeding onto the golden. Add a tablespoon of olive oil to each pouch, and vacuum seal.

3. Lightly season the ears of corn with a little smoked sea salt. Put them side-by-side in a large (1 gallon/3.8 liter) cooking pouch and vacuum seal.

4. Submerge all the pouches of vegetables in the water oven to cook for 30 minutes.

5. Remove the pouches from the water oven and submerge them in an ice water bath (half ice/half water) for an additional 20 minutes.

6. Meanwhile, make the yuzu emulsion by putting all emulsion ingredients into a food processor and blending until smooth.

7. Remove the beets from their pouches and gently blot off the excess oil.

8. Cut the corn from the cob and hold in a small bowl until it's time to assemble the salad.

For the lobster

2 (8-ounce/250-g) lobster tails, meat removed from shell

2 tablespoons (30 ml) unsalted butter (preferably European-style)

4 drops yuzu juice

$^1/_2$ teaspoon (2.5 ml) fennel pollen (plus a bit for finishing)

2 pinches sea salt (plus a bit for finishing)

1 pinch cracked black pepper

For the summer vegetable salad

2 medium golden beets

2 medium candy striped beets

2 tablespoons (30 ml) extra virgin olive oil

3 ears of corn, shucked and clean

$^1/_2$ teaspoon (2.5 ml) smoked sea salt

For the yuzu emulsion

$^1/_2$ tablespoon (7.5 ml) shallot

$^1/_2$ teaspoon (2.5 ml) ginger root

1 tablespoon (15 ml) raw agave syrup

6 tablespoons (90 ml) extra virgin olive oil

2 tablespoons (30 ml) yuzu juice (perhaps more depending on the brand)

1 teaspoon (5 ml) tarragon

2 large basil leaves

Fleur de sel and cracked pepper to taste

For plating

1 cup (3 oz/87 g) fennel bulb, sliced very thinly

$^1/_2$ cup (1.8 oz/52 g) English cucumber, sliced very thinly

12 heirloom cherry tomatoes, cut in half (grape tomatoes are fine if heirlooms aren't available)

4 cups (4 oz/118 g) assorted mixed greens

lobster tail with vegetable salad

continued from page 149

9. Thinly slice the beets on a mandolin just prior to tossing the salad, as the beets tend to oxidize and will turn brown if sliced too early.

Finish the salad and plate

1. Toss the beets, corn, fennel, cucumber, tomatoes, and mixed greens in a non-reactive bowl with the yuzu emulsion.

2. Arrange the salad on each plate as the bed of the dish.

3. Cut the lobster tails into thin medallions and arrange them on the salad.

4. Strategically place some tomatoes around the perimeter of the plate for eye catching edible garnish.

5. Drizzle a little olive oil and a light dusting of the fennel pollen and sea salt over the lobster, and serve.

porcini-mushroom-dusted salmon

Courtesy of Chef Lenard Rubin

Serves 4
Cooking time: 1 hour

Cook the salmon

1. Fill and preheat the water oven to 140°F (60°C).

2. Season the salmon fillets with salt and pepper; liberally sprinkle the presentation surface with porcini powder.

3. Put each fillet into a cooking pouch and gently vacuum seal.

4. Submerge the pouches in the water oven and cook for 45 minutes.

Make the fruit gastrique

1. Put all ingredients, except salt and pepper, into a small sauce pot.

2. Reduce until syrupy.

3. Season with salt and pepper.

Make the morel mushroom-clam sauce

1. On the stove top, heat oil in a saucepan, add garlic and shallot, and cook until caramelized.

2. Add the port and cook another minute.

3. Add clams in the shell and the crushed morel mushrooms and cook until the port is slightly reduced.

4. Add the demi-glace and reduce the mixture by half.

5. Add the cream and reduce by half again.

6. Strain into another small pot. Add the shucked clams, morel mushrooms, and butter and whisk until incorporated.

7. Season to taste with salt and pepper.

Make the strudel

1. Heat the traditional oven to 450°F (230°C).

2. Cut all mushrooms into small pieces.

3. Heat the olive oil in a pan over medium heat, add mushrooms, and cook, stirring frequently until browned.

For the salmon

4 (2½-oz/70-g each) salmon fillets

Salt and ground black pepper, to taste

4 tablespoons (60 ml) porcini powder

4 tablespoons (60 ml) olive oil

1 lemon (juice only)

For the prickly pear cactus fruit gastrique

½ cup (4 oz/120 ml) prickly pear cactus fruit purée

2 tablespoons (30 ml) agave syrup

2 tablespoons (30 ml) cider vinegar

1 teaspoon (5 ml) lemon juice

Salt and ground black pepper, to taste

For the morel mushroom-clam sauce

1 tablespoon (15 ml) olive oil

½ clove garlic, peeled and chopped

½ shallot, peeled and chopped

1 cup (8 oz/240 ml) port wine

6 each littleneck clams, in the shell

1 tablespoon (15 ml) dried morel mushrooms, crushed

½ cup (4 oz/120 ml) demi-glace

½ cup (4 oz/120 ml) heavy cream

9 morel mushrooms, cleaned

9 little neck clams, shucked

1 tablespoon (14 g) unsalted butter

Salt and ground black pepper, to taste

For the crab and goat cheese strudel

3 shiitake mushrooms

½ portobello mushroom

1 cluster oyster mushrooms

3 tablespoons (45 ml) olive oil

3 tablespoons (45 ml) demi-glace

¼ cup (2 oz/57 g) crab meat

continued on page 152

porcini-mushroom-dusted salmon

continued from page 151

1 tablespoon (15 ml) chives, chopped

Salt and ground black pepper, to taste

2 sheets phyllo dough

$1/2$ cup (4 oz/115 g) unsalted butter, clarified, melted

$1/4$ cup (2 oz/57 g) goat cheese

For plating

1 ounce (28 g) micro greens

Salt and ground black pepper, to taste

continued from page 147

4. Add the demi-glace and continue to cook until reduced slightly.

5. Remove from heat and add crab meat, chives, salt and pepper

6. Lay out one sheet of phyllo, brush with butter, and fold in half vertically. Brush the folded phyllo with butter again.

7. Lay the next phyllo sheet on top and brush with butter and fold vertically so that you now have a four-layered square.

8. Brush the surface with butter and spread the goat cheese in a thin line across the bottom of the phyllo square.

9. Put the mushroom-crab mixture over the line of goat cheese.

10. Starting at the bottom, roll the phyllo over the mushroom, crab, goat cheese mixture to make a cigar shape.

11. Cut the 'cigar' into 3 equal pieces.

12. Arrange the pieces on a small baking pan and bake in the oven and bake for 4 minutes, until golden.

Finish the salmon

1. Remove the salmon from the cooking pouches and pat dry.

2. On the stove top, heat the olive in a sauté pan and when hot, add the salmon, porcini powder side down, and cook until the fish turns a nice golden to dark brown color, about 2 minutes.

3. Remove the salmon from the pan and squeeze fresh lemon juice over it.

4. Spoon some mushroom-clam sauce around plate.

5. Place a piece of the wild mushroom, crab and goat cheese strudel in the middle of the sauce.

6. Lean a piece of salmon on the strudel.

7. Drizzle the fruit gastrique around the salmon and garnish with micro greens.

lemon and paprika sockeye salmon

Courtesy of Chef Sean Heather

Serves 4
Cooking time: 20 minutes

1. Fill and preheat the water oven to 125°F (52°C).

2. In a bowl, combine salt, sugar, and warm water, stirring well to dissolve. Chill well.

3. Put the salmon into the chilled brine for 20 minutes.

4. In a separate small bowl combine the marinade ingredients.

5. Remove the salmon from the brine, rinse, pat dry, and coat with the marinade.

6. Put the fillets, two to a pouch, into cooking pouches and vacuum seal.

7. Submerge the pouches in the water bath to cook for 15 to 20 minutes.

8. When cooked, gently remove the fillets from the pouches and garnish with freshly chopped parsley.

$^1/_3$ cup (3.5 oz/100 g) salt

$^1/_4$ cup (2.5 oz/70 g) sugar

4 cups (32 oz/1 liter) warm water

4 (5-oz/142-g each) sockeye salmon fillets

For the marinade

2 lemons, for zest (save juice for another use)

1 tablespoon(15 ml) smoked paprika

2 tablespoons (30 ml) olive oil

$^1/_4$ teaspoon (1.25 ml) freshly ground black pepper

For plating

Chopped fresh parsley, for garnish

maple-soy-cured salmon belly

Courtesy of Stephane Lemangnen

Serves 4
Cooking time: 45 minutes

Cure the salmon belly

1. Combine the soy sauce and the maple syrup in a small bowl.

2. Put the salmon belly into a zip-closure bag and pour the mixture over it.

3. Seal the bag and marinate, refrigerated, for 24 hours.

Cook the salmon belly

1. Fill and preheat the water oven to 122°F (50°C).

2. Remove the salmon from the marinade; discard the marinade.

3. Put the salmon belly into a cooking pouch and vacuum seal. (Vacuum on gentle/low if your sealer has this setting.)

4. Submerge the pouch in the water oven and cook for 20 minutes.

Prepare the stir-fry

1. In a stir-fry pan, heat some peanut oil.

2. In a bowl, combine the blanched soy beans, the boiled peanuts and the shimeji mushrooms.

3. Season with salt and pepper, and stir-fry for 30 seconds.

4. Add the pickled eggplant and cook for a few seconds more.

5. Set aside and keep warm until ready to serve.

Prepare the vinaigrette

1. Combine the rice vinegar, maple syrup, soy sauce, and grated ginger in a small bowl.

2. Add the peanut oil, whisk until emulsified, and set aside.

Finish the dish

1. Prepare a charcoal grill outdoors or in a very well-ventilated place.

2. Remove the salmon from the cooking pouch and grill until nicely caramelized on the outside.

3. Sprinkle with fleur de sel and serve with the soy bean stir-fry and soy-ginger vinaigrette on the side.

1 pound (16 oz/454 g) King salmon belly

$1/_4$ cup (2 oz/60 ml) dark amber maple syrup

$1/_4$ cup (2 oz/60 ml) soy sauce

For the stir-fry

2 tablespoons (60 ml) peanut oil

4 ounces (114 g) soy beans, blanched

4 ounces (114 g) boiled peanuts

4 ounces (114 g) shimeji mushrooms

Salt and pepper to taste

Pickled eggplant (found at Japanese markets)

For the soy-ginger vinaigrette

$1/_4$ cup (2 oz/60 ml) rice vinegar

3 tablespoons (45 ml) maple syrup

$1/_4$ cup (2 oz/60 ml) soy sauce

1-inch (2.5-cm) piece fresh ginger, peeled and finely grated

$1/_2$ cup (8 oz/120 ml) peanut oil

For finishing

Charcoal grill

Binchō-tan charcoal

Fleur de sel

porky rose scallops

Courtesy of Chef Jamie Watson

Serves 2
Cooking time: 1 hour

Prepare the toasted spicy rub

1. In a skillet over medium heat, toast the fennel and coriander seeds, peppercorns, and pepper flakes briefly.

2. Put the toasted spices into a spice grinder along with the chili powder, salt, and cinnamon and pulverize.

3. Store in a zip-closure bag or airtight container.

Cook the scallops

1. Fill and preheat the water oven to 140°F (60°C).

2. Remove side muscle from scallops and dry thoroughly.

3. Sprinkle scallops with toasted spicy rub and kosher salt.

4. Arrange scallops in a single layer in a cooking pouch. Add the bacon, rosemary and butter, and gently vacuum seal. (Avoid pulling a tight vacuum seal, which will deform the shape of the scallops.)

5. Submerge the pouch in the water bath to cook for 45 minutes.

6. Open the pouch and drain the accumulated pouch liquid into a saucepan and, over medium high heat, reduce by half.

7. Meanwhile, remove the scallops, bacon, and rosemary from the pouch and pat dry.

8. On the stove top, preheat a sauté pan and cook the bacon briefly to crisp. Remove and reserve.

9. Reduce heat to medium-high, coat the pan with a bit of high-smoke-point oil, and quickly sear the scallops on one side to color the surface.

10. Plate the scallops and bacon on a warmed plate and drizzle with the reduced sauce. Garnish with rosemary.

For the toasted spicy rub

$1/8$ cup (1 oz/30 g) fennel seeds

$1^1/_2$ teaspoons (7.5 ml) coriander seeds

$1^1/_2$ teaspoons (7.5 ml) peppercorns

$3/_4$ teaspoon (3.5 ml) red pepper flakes

$1/8$ cup (1 oz/30 g) chile powder (hot or mild as you like)

1 tablespoon (15 ml) kosher salt

1 tablespoon (15 ml) ground cinnamon

For the scallops

8 (2 oz/54 g each) fresh diver scallops

2 teaspoons (10 ml) spicy rub

Kosher salt

2 slices (2 oz/54 g) apple wood smoked bacon

1 sprig fresh rosemary, plus some for garnish

1 teaspoon (5 ml) unsalted butter

1 tablespoon (15 ml) high-smoke-point oil

sea scallops with COUSCOUS

Courtesy of Chef Josh Horrigan

Serves 4
Cooking time: 30 minutes

1. Fill and preheat the water oven to 122°F (50°C).

2. Lightly season the scallops with sea salt, cracked black pepper, and saffron.

3. Arrange the scallops in a single layer in a cooking pouch, add a tablespoon of butter to each pouch, and gently vacuum seal.

3. Submerge the pouch in the water bath to cook for 30 minutes.

Make the couscous

1. On the stove top, bring the water to a boil, add the couscous, cover and remove from the heat.

2. Let sit for 5 minutes, until all liquid is absorbed.

Finish the scallops

1. In a shallow bowl, combine the flour with salt and pepper to taste.

2. Heat a heavy cast iron skillet to medium high heat and add the clarified butter.

3. Remove the scallops from the pouch (save the liquid in the pouch) and lightly dredge both sides of each scallop in the seasoned flour.

4. Sear the scallops on each side just long enough to brown.

5. Drain the scallops on paper towels to pull away moisture.

Finish the couscous

1. Fluff the couscous with a fork.

2. Add some of the scallop pouch liquor and all remaining ingredients.

3. Season with salt and pepper to taste.

Plate

1. Toss the microgreens with a bit of the lemon oil, salt and pepper.

2. Center a ring mold in the plate and pack tightly with the couscous. Carefully remove the mold.

3. Arrange three scallops around the couscous, drizzle the plate with lemon oil, garnish with microgreens.

12 U-10 dry-packed diver sea scallops

Kosher sea salt

Cracked black pepper

2 pinches saffron

$\frac{1}{2}$ cup (2 oz/60 g) Wondra flour

2 tablespoons (30 g) clarified butter

For the couscous

1 cup (8 oz/240 ml) water

1 cup (5.3 oz/150 g) couscous

Sous vide scallop pouch liquor

1 tablespoon (15 ml) minced mint leaves

1 tablespoon (15 ml) finely minced sweet Italian basil

1 pinch saffron

$\frac{1}{4}$ cup (0.5 oz/13 g) oil-packed, sun-dried tomatoes, finely sliced

1 teaspoon (5 ml) oil from the sun-dried tomatoes

Sea salt and cracked black pepper to taste

For plating

Microgreens, for garnish (micro-basil and micro-arugula work well)

2 tablespoons (30 ml) high-quality Meyer lemon oil plus a bit for the greens

octopus, relish and corn pudding

Courtesy of Chef Jason Wilson

Serves 6
Cooking time: 8½ hours

Prepare the pickled green tomato relish 24 hours ahead

1. Put the tomatoes into a large non-reactive bowl or large (1 gallon/3.8 liter) zip-closure pouch.

2. In a saucepan over medium heat, mix together all remaining ingredients and simmer for 5 minutes to dissolve them and infuse their flavors.

3. Remove the mixture from the heat and cool for 10 minutes.

4. Pour the mixture through a strainer over the green tomatoes. Cover the bowl, or evacuate the air from the pouch (page 11) and seal.

5. Refrigerate and allow 24 hours for the tomatoes to pickle.

Cook the octopus

1. Fill and preheat the water oven to 156°F (69°C).

2. Thoroughly wash the octopi; if using tentacles, cut them into bite-size pieces. Put them into a large bowl and set aside.

3. In a saucepan, over medium-high heat, make a marinade by combining all remaining ingredients, and simmer for 5 minutes.

4. Purée the marinade until smooth and pour it over the octopus, tossing to coat.

5. Arrange the octopi or tentacle pieces in a single, even layer in one or two large (1 gallon/3.8 liter) cooking pouches, fold over the end of the pouch, and secure with a clip.

6. Chill the pouch for 30 minutes in the freezer to firm the marinade for sealing.

7. Vacuum seal the pouches, submerge them in the water bath, and cook for 8 hours.

For the pickled green tomato relish

4 cups (25 oz/720 g) green tomatoes, diced large

3 tablespoons (45 ml) kosher salt

2 tablespoons (30 ml) white sugar

1 teaspoon (5 ml) ground cumin

1 teaspoon (5 ml) coriander

1 tablespoon (15 ml) juniper berries

1 teaspoon (5 ml) fennel seeds

1 teaspoon (5 ml) cloves

1 teaspoon (5ml) chile flakes

6 cloves garlic, peeled and smashed

2 cups (16 oz/454 ml) cider vinegar

6 branches fresh mint

For the octopus

30 baby octopi or 6 octopus tentacles, 4 to 5 inches (10 to 12 cm) each

¼ cup (2 oz/60 ml) olive oil

6 cloves garlic, peeled and smashed

1 tablespoon (15 ml) fresh orange zest

1 tablespoon (15 ml) kosher salt

1 teaspoon (5 ml) ground cumin

1 teaspoon (5 ml) pimentón (ground Spanish paprika)

1 teaspoon (5 ml) ground coriander

1 teaspoon (5 ml) chile flakes

6 stems Italian flat leaf parsley

continued on page 162

octopus, relish and corn pudding

continued from page 161

Make the white corn pudding

1. In a saucepan over medium heat, combine the chicken stock, shallots, nutmeg, coriander, bay leaves and salt, and simmer for 2 minutes.

2. Add the corn kernels and crème fraîche and continue to simmer for 10 minutes more, stirring constantly.

3. With a hand (immersion) blender, purée all ingredients well.

4. Add the fresh herbs and continue to purée until fairly smooth.

5. Add the corn juice and cook for 15 minutes over low heat, or until the mixture reaches a pudding consistency.

6. Adjust the seasoning and keep warm on the stove top. *Alternately, keep warm in a water oven preheated to 140°F (60°C). To do so, transfer the pudding to a large (1 gallon/3.8 liter) zip-closure cooking pouch, evacuate the air (page 11) and seal. Submerge the pouch in the water bath until needed.*

Finish the octopus and plate

1. Remove the octopus from the pouches and quickly grill or sauté to finish.

2. On the serving plate, center a mound of pickled green tomatoes.

3. Arrange several octopi or the pieces of one tentacle atop the relish.

4. Garnish the plate with a swoosh of the white corn pudding.

162

continued from page 161

For the white corn pudding

$1/2$ cup (4 oz/120 ml) chicken stock

1 ounce (28 g) shallots, peeled and chopped

$1^1/_2$ teaspoons (7.5 ml) ground nutmeg

$1^1/_2$ teaspoons (7.5 ml) ground coriander

2 bay leaves

$1^1/_2$ teaspoons (7.5 ml) kosher salt, or to taste

32 ounces (907 g) white corn kernels

8 ounces (227 g) crème fraîche

4 stems fresh tarragon, stripped for leaves

2 to 4 stems lemon thyme, stripped for leaves

2 cups (16 oz/454 ml) fresh white corn juice*

* *To make fresh corn juice, purée 1 cup fresh kernels with 1 cup water until smooth.*

halibut beurre rouge

Courtesy of Chef Phillip Foss

Serves 4
Cooking time: 30 minutes

Cook the heirloom potatoes

1. Preheat the traditional oven to 450°F (230°C).

2. Wash the potatoes under cold water and transfer to paper toweling to dry.

3. In a mixing bowl, toss the potatoes with the oil, thyme, salt and pepper.

4. Transfer the potatoes to a foil lined baking sheet and cover completely with another sheet of aluminum foil.

5. Cook in the oven for 25 minutes or until potatoes are tender.

6. Remove from foil and keep warm.

Cook the halibut

1. Fill and preheat the water oven to 132°F (55.5°C).

2. Season the halibut on both sides with salt.

3. Put the fillets, two to a pouch, into small (1 quart/0.9 liter) cooking pouches, along with the butter and sprigs of thyme and vacuum seal.

4. Submerge the pouches in the water bath and cook for 20 minutes.

Make the shaved asparagus and vinaigrette

1. Using a vegetable peeler, carefully peel the asparagus to create long shavings.

2. To make the balsamic vinaigrette, whisk together a good balsamic vinegar, salt and pepper, then whisk in the olive oil in a slow steady stream. Set aside.

Cook the morels

1. Heat a small sauté pan over medium heat and melt the butter.

2. Add the shallots and cook until translucent.

3. Add the morels and sweat until tender, about 5 minutes.

4. Season to taste with salt and pepper, and hold warm until plating.

For the heirloom potatoes

1 pound (16 oz/450 g) heirloom potatoes (Bintje or similar)

2 ounces (60 ml) olive oil

5 sprigs thyme

Salt and fresh cracked black pepper to taste

For the halibut

4 (6 oz/180 g each) halibut fillets

1 stick (4 oz/113 g) unsalted butter

Salt, to taste

4 sprigs thyme

For the shaved asparagus

2 green asparagus

2 purple asparagus

1 tablespoon (15 ml) good balsamic vinegar

Salt and fresh cracked black pepper

3 tablespoons (45 ml) olive oil

For the morels

2 ounces (57 g) unsalted butter

2 shallots, chopped

8 ounces (227 g) fresh morels, trimmed and well washed

Salt and pepper to taste

For the beurre rouge

8 ounces (240 ml) red wine

1 tablespoon (15 ml) shallot, finely minced

3 sprigs thyme

1 ounce (30 ml) sauce meurette or cream

2 sticks (8 oz/227 g) unsalted butter, cubed and chilled

Salt and fresh cracked black pepper to taste

halibut beurre rouge

continued from page 163

Make the beurre rouge

1. In a non-reactive sauce pot over medium-high heat, pour the wine and add the shallots and thyme sprigs, and cook until reduced to a syrup-like consistency.

2. Add the sauce meurette (or cream) and reduce by half.

3. Reduce the heat to low and, using a wire whisk, incorporate a couple of cubes of the butter, whisking continuously until the butter has melted.

4. Gradually add more butter using the same technique until all of the butter has been incorporated.

5. Strain through a fine meshed strainer and keep warm (but not hot) until ready to plate.
Alternatively, pour the sauce into a zip-closure cooking pouch, remove the air (page 11) and zip the seal. Submerge the pouch in the water oven to keep warm as the halibut cooks.

Plate

1. Lightly and gently toss the asparagus shavings in the balsamic vinaigrette and season to taste.

2. Arrange the heirloom potatoes in the center of heated plates and spoon the beurre rouge around them.

3. Scatter a few morels around the dish.

4. Remove the halibut from the pouches and very gently place a fillet atop the potatoes.

5. Gently position a pile of shaved asparagus atop the halibut and serve.

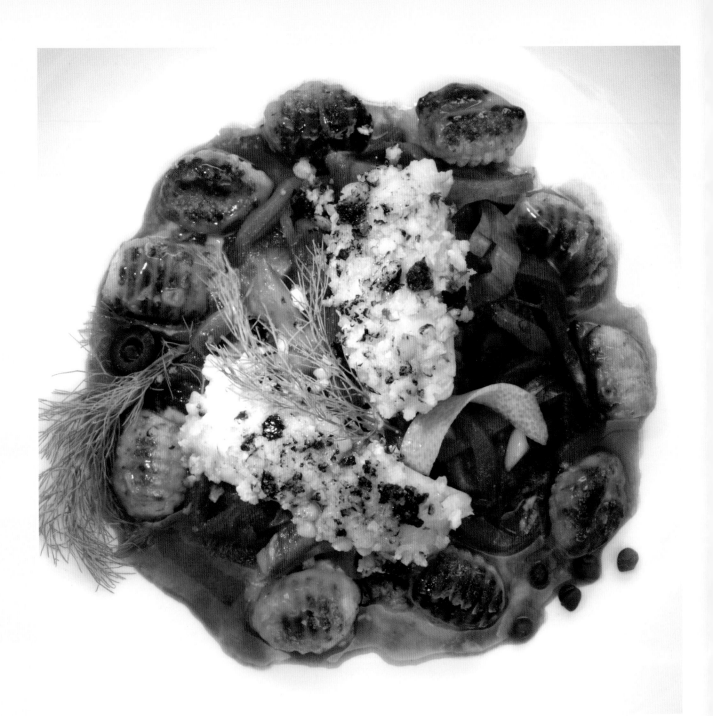

sole with fennel and pepper stew

Courtesy of Chef Alex Seidel

Serves 4
Cooking time: 2 hours

Note: Soak the salt cod in water in the refrigerator for 2 days before making the gnocchi.

Prepare the potato brandade gnocchi

1. Fill and preheat the water oven to 180°F (82°C).

2. Put the potatoes into large (1 gallon/3.8 liter) cooking pouches and vacuum seal.

3. Submerge the pouches in the water bath to cook for 30 to 45 minutes, until tender when pressed through the pouch.

4. Meanwhile, rinse the salt cod under cold water.

5. In a saucepan over low heat, combine the cod, blanched garlic, milk, and enough water to cover; bring to a simmer and cook for 15 minutes.

6. Strain off the liquid, reserving the solids for step 7.

7. In a stand mixer, fitted with a paddle attachment, process the fish mixture on slow to medium speed until the fish is broken to rice-sized flakes. Reserve warm.

8. Open the potato pouches, drain off the liquid, and run the potatoes through a food mill.

9. Put the potatoes into a large mixing bowl, sprinkle the cod mixture over them, and then add flour, eggs and olive oil, and season with salt and pepper.

10. Gently work the mixture with a wooden spoon until the dough just begins to come together.

11. Pour the mixture out onto a flat surface and divide into quarters.

12. Roll out each quarter into a long snake-shaped roll, dusting often with flour to avoid sticking, and cut the rolls into 1-inch (2.5-cm) pillows.

13. If not using immediately, put the gnocchi pillows in a single layer into large (1 gallon/3.8 liter) cooking pouches and seal only; do not vacuum or you will crush them. Store in the freezer up to 3 days.

For the potato brandade gnocchi

4 ounces (120 g) salt cod

1 pound Yukon gold potatoes, peeled and diced to 1 inch (2.5 cm)

4 cloves garlic, peeled and blanched in milk to cover 3 times

1 cup (8 oz/240 ml) whole milk

$1\frac{1}{2}$ to 2 cups (6.75-9 oz/199-266 g) all-purpose flour

4 egg yolks

3 tablespoons (45 ml) olive oil

Salt and white pepper, to taste

2 tablespoons (30 ml) grapeseed oil

2 tablespoons (30 ml) butter

$1\frac{1}{2}$ to 2 cups (12 to 16 oz/ 355 to 473 ml) water

For the fennel and pepper stew

2 tablespoons (30 ml) grapeseed oil

1 bulb fennel, stalks removed, sliced julienne, fronds reserved

1 red bell pepper, stemmed, seeded, and sliced julienne

1 yellow bell pepper, stemmed, seeded, and sliced julienne

1 red onion, peeled and sliced julienne

1 yellow onion, peeled and sliced julienne

2 cloves garlic, peeled and thinly sliced

16 ounces (473 g) San Marzano tomatoes, for juice only (squeeze juice out of whole tomatoes, reserve tomatoes for another use)

Salt and white pepper, to taste

1 teaspoon (5 ml) parsley

$\frac{1}{8}$ teaspoon (0.6 ml) red chile pepper flakes

1 tablespoon (15 ml) red wine vinegar

continued on page 168

sole with fennel and pepper stew

continued from page 167

14. Before plating, sear the gnocchi in a sauté pan over medium heat in grapeseed oil until golden on both sides. (Gnocchi may be seared from frozen.)

15. Add the butter and enough water to cover the gnocchi. Continue to cook until the gnocchi rise to the surface of the water, about 1 minute more.

16. Strain off the liquid, and reserve the gnocchi in a bowl.

Cook the fennel and pepper stew

1. In a large pot over low heat, warm the oil; add the fennel, peppers, onions and garlic and sweat until tender.

2. Add the tomato juice, bring to boil, then turn down to simmer for 30 minutes.

3. Season with salt, pepper, parsley, red chile flakes and red wine vinegar.

4. Reserve warm.

Cook the petrale sole

1. Reset the water oven temperature to 143°F (61.5°C). To speed the process along, remove 1 to 2 quarts/liters of hot water from the water bath with a large measuring cup and replace it with an equivalent amount of ice water. Preheat the traditional oven to 400°F (204°C.)

2. In a bowl, prepare the crust by mixing the olives, bread crumbs, pine nuts, and parsley; season with salt and pepper to taste. Set aside.

3. Season the filets with a bit of salt and pepper.

4. Tear 4 sheets of plastic wrap about 12 inches long and have ready.

5. Working with one filet at a time, roulade (roll) each portion of fish along its length and wrap tightly in the plastic wrap to hold the shape.

6. Put the fish roulades into a small (1 quart/0.9 liter) cooking pouch and vacuum seal.

7. Submerge the pouch in the water bath to cook for 8 minutes and remove. If not finishing right away, quick chill the pouch submerged in ice water (half ice, half water) for 5 minutes and refrigerate for up to 24 hours.

continued from page 167

For the black olive crusted sole

12 to 14 (2.8 oz/84g) sun-dried black olives, roughly chopped

$1/4$ cup (0.5 oz/14 g) panko bread crumbs

$1/4$ cup (1 oz/30 g) pine nuts, roughly chopped

1 teaspoon (5 ml) parsley, chopped

Salt and white pepper, to taste

4 (5.5 oz/163 g) portions petrale sole

$1/4$ cup (2 oz/60 ml) grapeseed oil

4 egg whites

For the beurre fondue

1 cup (8 oz/240 ml) dry white wine

1 tablespoon (15 ml) white wine vinegar

1 sprig thyme

6 white peppercorns

2 small shallots, peeled and sliced

$1/2$ cup (4 oz/120 ml) heavy cream

1 stick (4 oz/113 g) unsalted butter

1 teaspoon (5 ml) lemon zest

2 tablespoons (30 ml) capers, rinsed and drained

Salt and white pepper, to taste

Fennel fronds, for garnish

168

Finish and plate

1. Remove the fish from the pouch, and remove and discard the plastic wrap.

2. Heat the oil in large sauté pan and sear the fish rolls until golden brown, presentation side down.

3. Flip them over, brush the presentation side with egg white and sprinkle liberally with the bread crumb mixture.

4. Transfer the pan to the traditional oven and bake for 4 to 5 minutes, or until the crust is golden brown.

5. Meanwhile, make the beurre fondue in a small sauce pot by combining the wine, vinegar, thyme, peppercorns and shallots.

6. Simmer to *au sec* (nearly dry), add the cream, bring back to a simmer, and allow the sauce to reduce to a thick and sticky consistency.

7. Slowly whisk butter into the mixture, a few cubes at a time, allowing it to melt before adding more.

8. Season with the lemon zest and capers and salt and pepper to taste.

9. Reserve warm.

10. Spoon a fourth of the fennel and pepper stew into each of four large entrée bowls.

11. Coat the potato brandade gnocchi in the beurre fondue and then spoon a few gnocchi around the stew in each bowl.

12. Place one filet in each bowl on top of the stew and garnish with fennel fronds.

sides

Brussels sprouts with pancetta

Serves 4 to 6
Cooking time: 1 to 1½ hours

1. Fill and preheat the water oven to 182–185°F (83–85°C).

2. Put the Brussels sprouts, butter, salt, and pepper into a large (1 gallon/3.78 liter) cooking pouch, and vacuum seal.

3. Submerge the pouch in the water bath, and cook for 1 to 1½ hours. (Check at 15 to 20 minutes to be sure the pouch is still fully submerged. Small amounts of air that remain between the sprouts might cause the pouch to float, which would result in uneven cooking. If the pouch floats, open the pouch and vacuum seal again to remove the air.)

4. In a small skillet, fry the pancetta over medium heat to render fat. Add the onion and garlic and sauté until they are translucent, about 5 to 6 minutes.

5. Remove the Brussels sprouts from the pouch, drain away any accumulated liquid, and put them into the skillet. Toss with the pancetta mixture to coat well.

6. Drizzle on the balsamic vinegar, toss again, and serve immediately.

1 pound (16 oz/454 g) Brussels sprouts, washed, trimmed and halved

2 tablespoons (30 ml) unsalted butter

½ teaspoon (2.5 ml) coarse salt

¼ teaspoon (1.25 ml) black pepper

4 ounces (113 g) diced pancetta or bacon, diced

½ small sweet onion, peeled and diced

2 cloves garlic, peeled and minced or pressed

1 to 2 teaspoons (5 to 10 ml) balsamic vinegar

crushed rutabaga

1 pound (16 oz/454 g) fresh rutabaga, peeled and diced

1½ tablespoon (22.5 ml) salt

1 tablespoon (30 ml) white pepper

2 teaspoons (10 ml) ground ginger

½ stick (2 oz/60 g) unsalted butter

Courtesy of Chef Richard Blais

Serves 6 to 8
Cooking time: 1 to 1½ hours

1. Fill and preheat the water oven to 182–185°F (83–85°C).

2. Vacuum seal all ingredients in a cooking pouch, keeping the rutabaga pieces in a single layer.

3. Submerge the pouch in the water oven and cook for 1 to 1½ hours.

4. Remove the pouch from the water oven, allow it to cool slightly, then coarsely mash the rutabaga through the cooking pouch using the flat back of the tines of a fork.

5. If not serving immediately, quick chill the rutabaga by submerging the pouch in an ice water bath (half ice, half water) for 30 to 40 minutes, then refrigerate for up to 48 hours.

6. To reheat, simply drop the cooking pouch into the water bath (along with the pouches of any other foods you may be re-warming) for at least 30 minutes, or until ready to serve.

cauliflower purée

1 large head cauliflower

$\frac{1}{2}$ teaspoon (2.5 ml) coarse salt

$\frac{1}{4}$ teaspoon (1.25 ml) freshly ground pepper

2 tablespoons (30 ml) butter, melted

2 to 3 tablespoons (30 to 45 ml) half-and-half or cream

Serves 4 to 6

Cooking time: 1 to 1½ hours

1. Fill and preheat the water oven to 182–185°F (83–85°C)..

2. Wash the cauliflower well and let drain to remove excess water.

3. Trim away the outer leaves with a sharp knife and slice the head in half and then the halves into ½-inch (1.25-cm) slices.

4. Sprinkle the cauliflower with the salt and pepper.

5. Divide the slices between two large (1 gallon/3.78 liter) cooking pouches, arranging them in a relatively even layer about an inch (2.5 cm) thick. Add a tablespoon (.5 oz/15 g) of butter to each pouch, and vacuum seal.

6. Put the pouches into the water bath to cook for 1 to 1½ hours. (Check the pouches at 15 to 20 minutes, because air remaining in the spaces between florets may cause them to float and result in uneven cooking. If the pouches float, remove them, cut open near the seal, vacuum seal again, and return the pouches to the water bath.)

7. Remove the pouches from the bath after the cooking time has elapsed, open them and drain the accumulated liquid, and pour the cauliflower into the work bowl of a food processor or blender.

8. Add a couple of tablespoons (1 oz/30 ml) of half-and-half and blend or process until smooth. Pulse or blend on low for short intervals, turn the machine off, remove the lid, and use a spatula to scrape down the sides and push the unblended pieces to the bottom. Replace the lid and blend again. Repeat until the purée is smooth and creamy. Add additional half-and-half by the tablespoon only if necessary to thin the purée to the desired consistency.

9. Taste and adjust seasonings, if desired, and serve immediately.

Alternately, quick chill the purée for later use

1. Put the purée in a clean zip-closure cooking pouch, evacuate the air (page 11), and seal.

2. Immerse the sealed pouch in an ice water bath (half ice, half water) for at least 30 minutes, then refrigerate for up to 48 hours.

3. Reheat the pouch in the water bath, along with any other items you may be warming, for 30 to 40 minutes or longer before serving.

onions with bacon and cinnamon

Courtesy of Chef Richard Blais

Serves 6 to 8
Cooking time: 1 to 1½ hours

1. Fill and preheat the water oven to 182–185°F (83–85°C).

2. Put all ingredients except the sage and thyme into a cooking pouch and vacuum seal.

3. Submerge in the water oven and cook for 1 to 1½ hours.

4. If not serving right away, quick chill the pouch in an ice water bath (half ice, half water) for at least 30 minutes, then refrigerate for up to 48 hours. Reheat in the water bath, along with any other items you may be warming, for 30 to 40 minutes or longer.

5. At serving time, remove the mixture from the pouch to a warmed serving dish, and finish with a sprinkle of chopped sage and thyme.

48 pearl onions, peeled, whole
1 slice (1 oz/ 30 g) bacon

½ teaspoon (2.5 ml) ground cinnamon

1 tablespoon (15 ml) unsalted butter

Fresh sage leaves, chopped, for garnish, if desired

Fresh thyme sprigs, stripped of leaves, for garnish, if desire

festive sweet potatoes

Courtesy of Chef Richard Blais

Serves 4 to 6
Cooking time: 1 to 1½ hours

1 pound (16 oz/454 g) sweet potatoes, peeled and diced

3 tablespoons (45 ml) maple syrup

1 tablespoon (15 ml) salt

2 teaspoons (10 ml) white pepper

2 teaspoons (10 ml) white truffle oil

Fresh sage leaves, chopped, for garnish

Parmesan cheese, grated, for garnish

1. Fill and preheat the water oven to 182–185°F (83–85°C).

2. Put all ingredients, except the truffle oil, sage leaves and Parmesan into a cooking pouch and vacuum seal.

3. Submerge the pouch in the water oven and cook for 1 to 1½ hours.

4. If not serving right away, quick chill the potatoes in their sealed pouch in an ice water bath (half ice, half water) for 30 to 40 minutes, then refrigerate for up to 2 days. Reheat in the water bath, along with any other items you may be warming, for 30 to 40 minutes or longer.

5. Remove sweet potatoes from the pouch, put them into a blender or food processor, add the truffle oil, and purée.

6. Spoon into a warmed bowl for serving. Garnish with chopped fresh sage and freshly grated Parmesan cheese, if desired.

rosemary and garlic new potatoes

Serves 4
Cooking time: 1½ to 2 hours

8 to 10 red skinned new potatoes

1 tablespoon (15 ml) olive oil

½ teaspoon (2.5 ml) sea salt

¼ teaspoon (1.25 ml) freshly ground black pepper

¼ teaspoon (1.25 ml) garlic powder

1 to 2 fresh rosemary sprigs

1 tablespoon (15 ml) bacon fat or unsalted butter

1. Fill and preheat the water oven to 182–185°F (83–85°C).

2. Wash the potatoes and pat dry. Cut each potato, skin on, into quarters.

3. Drizzle the potatoes with a little olive oil and stir them to coat evenly.

4. Season the potatoes with a sprinkling of salt, pepper, and garlic powder.

5. Strip the leaves from the rosemary sprigs; finely mince them and sprinkle onto the potatoes.

6. Put a tablespoon of rendered bacon fat (or unsalted butter) into a cooking pouch, add the seasoned potatoes in a single layer, and vacuum seal. Do not overfill the pouch.

7. Submerge the pouch in the water bath and cook for a minimum of 1½ to 2 hours. Be sure that the food is entirely submerged below the surface of the water.

8. Open the pouch and serve immediately, or quick chill in an ice water bath (half ice, half water), and refrigerate for up to 48 hours. Reheat to use as a side dish or in soups, or use directly from the refrigerator in potato salad or wraps.

potato salad

Serves 4 to 6
Cooking time: 45 to 90 minutes

1. Fill and preheat the water oven to 183°F (84°C).

2. Cut the potatoes in half or in quarters (dependent on size) and season them lightly with salt and pepper.

3. Put the potatoes into a large (1 gallon/3.8 liter) cooking pouch and vacuum seal.

4. Submerge the pouch in the water oven and cook for 45 to 90 minutes. If not serving right away, quick chill the potatoes in their pouch, submerged in ice water (half ice, half water) for 20 to 30 minutes, then refrigerate for up to 2 days.

5. When ready to proceed, make a dressing in a small bowl, adding all dressing ingredients except the olive oil. Whisk to combine and let the mixture sit for 10 to 15 minutes or longer for the flavors to marry. Just before serving whisk in the olive oil slowly to finish the dressing.

6. Drain the potatoes and put them into a larger bowl.

7. Add all remaining herbs and vegetables, pour on the dressing, and toss to coat. Check seasonings and adjust salt and pepper to your liking, and serve.

For the vegetables

$1\frac{1}{2}$ pounds (24 oz/680 g) red fingerling potatoes

Salt and pepper to taste

$\frac{1}{2}$ red pepper, cored and diced

1 stalk celery, chopped

3 green onions, trimmed, green and white parts chopped

2 tablespoons (30 ml) minced flat leaf parsley

For the dressing

1 tablespoon (15 ml) white wine vinegar

$\frac{1}{4}$ teaspoon (1.25 ml) garlic powder

$\frac{1}{4}$ teaspoon (1.25 ml) onion powder

$\frac{1}{8}$ teaspoon (0.6 ml) cayenne pepper or to taste

1 teaspoon honey or $\frac{1}{2}$ packet sucralose, stevia, or your preferred sweetener

3 tablespoons (45 ml) extra virgin olive oil

butter-poached red kuri squash

Courtesy of Chef Michael Solomonov

Serves 4
Cooking time: 2 hours

1. In a bowl, sprinkle the squash with the salt, toss to coat, and let it sit at room temperature for 3 hours.

2. Fill and preheat the water oven to 158°F (70°C).

3. Wipe the salt from the squash and toss with the sugar.

4. Put the seasoned squash in a single layer into a large (1 gallon/3.8 liter) cooking pouch. Add the butter and vacuum seal.

5. Submerge the pouch in the water bath and cook for 2 hours.

6. When ready to serve, transfer the squash from the pouch to a serving bowl and toss with sesame seeds and black pepper.

1 (4 lb/450 g) red kuri squash, peeled, seeded, and cut into wedges or large cubes

$1/3$ cup (2 oz/57 g) kosher salt

$1/4$ cup (2 oz/57 g) unrefined sugar

1 stick (4 oz/114 g) unsalted butter, browned and refrigerated

2 tablespoons (30 ml) white sesame seeds

Coarsely ground black pepper, to taste

183

corn on the cob

4 whole fresh ears of corn (cut in half if serving 8)

Salt and pepper to taste

2 tablespoons (30 ml) butter

Serves 4 to 8
Cooking time: 45 to 90 minutes

1. Fill and preheat the water oven to 182°F (83.5°C).

2. Put ears in a single layer in a large (1 gallon/3.8 liter) food-grade cooking pouch, season to taste with salt and pepper, add the butter and vacuum seal.

3. Submerge the pouch in the water oven and cook for 45 to 90 minutes.

4. Remove the corn from the water oven and, if serving right away, open the pouch and enjoy or, if desired, give the ears a quick turn on a hot grill (30 seconds per side) just to add a few grill marks and smoky flavor before serving.

5. If not serving immediately, remove from the water oven, quick chill by submerging the pouch in ice water (half ice, half water), and refrigerate for up to 48 hours.

6. Reheat in the pouch in the water oven at 130°F or higher for 20 minutes before serving, followed by step 4 (above).

desserts

key lime pie

Courtesy of Vicky McDonald

Serves 8
Cooking time: 30 minutes

1. Fill and preheat the water oven to 180°F (82°C).

2. Whisk all the filling ingredients together into a medium-sized bowl, until well combined.

3. Pour the filling into a large (1 gallon/3.8 liter) zip-closure cooking pouch, evacuate the air (page 11), and zip closed.

4. Submerge the pouch in the water bath to cook for 30 minutes.

Make the crust

1. Grease an 8-inch (20-cm) round spring form pan/tin with a little butter.

2. In a large bowl, mix together the graham cracker crumbs, sugar and melted butter with a spoon.

3. Press the crust mixture evenly into the base of the prepared pan/tin, using the back of a spoon.

4. Put the crust into the refrigerator to harden.

Assemble the pie

1. After the filling has cooked for 30 minutes, remove it from the water bath and massage the contents through the pouch to 'stir'.

2. Open the pouch and pour the key lime filling onto the hardened graham cracker crust.

3. Allow to cool at room temperature for about 30 minutes, then refrigerator for at least 2 hours.

Make the topping

1. Beat the heavy whipping cream to soft peaks.

2. Put the whipped cream into a piping bag with a medium tip/nozzle.

3. Pipe small circles of cream around the edge of the pie and one large circle in the center.

4. Arrange thin slices of key lime on top of the pie.

For the key lime filling

$\frac{1}{2}$ cup (4 oz/120 ml) key lime juice, from fresh key limes

1 (14-oz/396-g) can sweetened condensed milk

4 egg yolks

For the crust

1 teaspoon (5 g) butter, to grease the tin

6 tablespoons (90 g) butter, melted

$1\frac{1}{2}$ cups (5 oz/150 g) graham cracker crumbs

2 tablespoons (30 ml) granulated white sugar

For the topping

$\frac{1}{2}$ cup (4 oz/120 ml) heavy whipping cream

2 extra key limes for decorating

pumpkin crème brûlée

Serves 4
Cooking time: 1 to 1½ hours

1. Elevate the bottom perforated grill of the water oven about 2 inches (5 cm), either on a sous vide baking platform or non-rusting, adjustable wire rack for roasting. Fill the ramekins you will use to cook your custard with water and position them on the perforated grill.

2. Fill the water oven with just enough water to come within ½ inch (1.27 cm) of the top of the ramekins. Remove ramekins, empty, and dry them well.

3. Liberally butter the insides of all the ramekins.

4. Preheat the water oven to 195°F (90.5°C).

5. In a medium bowl, beat the eggs until light yellow. Add the heavy cream, pumpkin purée, brown sugar, vanilla extract, cinnamon, and nutmeg, and beat again to mix well.

6. Pour the pumpkin mixture into each ramekin, almost to the top, and cover with foil.

7. Carefully place each filled ramekin into the heated water bath. Cook the custards for at least 1 hour and up to 1½ hours.

8. Remove the ramekins from the water bath, cool to room temperature, and refrigerate for several hours or overnight. Bring back to room temperature before serving.

9. At serving, sprinkle each serving with ½ teaspoon (2.5 ml) brown sugar and caramelize the topping with a kitchen torch or under a preheated broiler.

1 to 2 tablespoons (15 to 30 ml) unsalted butter (for greasing ramekins)

4 egg yolks

¾ cup (6 oz/180 ml) heavy cream

¾ cup (5.75 oz/163 g) pumpkin purée

⅓ cup (2.55 oz/73 g) light brown sugar

¼ teaspoon (1.25 ml) pure vanilla extract

⅛ teaspoon (0.625 ml) ground cinnamon

1 pinch grated nutmeg

4 tablespoons (60 ml) brown sugar for finishing

Masala chai crème brûlée

Courtesy of Chef Sam Hussain

Serves 4
Cooking time: 30 minutes

1. Fill and preheat the water oven to 183°F (84°C).

2. Put the cardamom pods, cinnamon sticks and bay leaves into a small muslin spice bag or tie in a square of cheesecloth.

3. Generously butter the interior of 4 ramekins and set aside.

4. Whisk (or blend) together the cream, egg yolks, sugar, and vanilla extract until well blended.

5. Put the cream mixture, tea bags, and spice bundle into a large (1 gallon/3.8 liter) zip-closure cooking pouch, evacuate the air (page 11), and zip the seal closed.

6. Submerge the pouch in the water bath to cook for 30 minutes. Agitate/shake the pouch half way through to ensure even cooking.

7. Remove the pouch from water bath and knead to distribute the liquid mixture evenly.

8. With scissors, cut a small corner off the pouch and pour the cream mixture evenly into the prepared ramekins. Discard the spice bundle and tea bags with the pouch.

9. Refrigerate for at least 4 hours (up to 8 hours is fine.)

10. When ready to serve, sprinkle each serving with 1 teaspoon (5 ml) brown sugar and caramelize with a kitchen torch or under a pre-heated broiler.

3 cardamom pods, lightly split

2 sticks (2 inches/5 cm each) cinnamon

3 bay leaves

Butter for greasing ramekins

2 cups (16 oz/473 ml) heavy cream

4 egg yolks

4 tablespoons (60 ml) sugar

1 teaspoon (5 ml) pure vanilla extract

2 Darjeeling tea bags (or loose tea, in an infuser)

4 teaspoons (20 ml) granulated or brown sugar (for finishing)

sago seed (tapioca) pudding

Courtesy of Chef Sam Hussain

Serves 4
Cooking time: 2 hours

1. Fill and preheat the water oven to 174°F (79°C).

2. Put all ingredients, except cream and slice almonds, into a zip-closure cooking pouch, evacuate the air (page 11), and seal.

3. Submerge the pouch and cook for 2 hours.

4. Remove from the water bath and massage the contents through the pouch to break up any lumps.

5. Pour the pudding into a large ramekin and top with swirl of heavy cream and sliced almonds.

$1/3$ cup (2.8 oz/80 g) sago seeds (tapioca pearls)

2 tablespoons (30 ml) sugar

1 star anise pod

3 bay leaves

3 cardamom pods (pierced)

12 ounces (355 ml) pasteurized whole milk

1 tablespoon (15 ml) coconut powder

2 ounces (60 ml) heavy cream

1 good pinch sliced almonds

ice cream with dulce de leche

Serves 8
Cooking time: 14 hours

Make the dulce de leche

1. Fill and preheat the water oven to 185°F (85°C).

2. Pour and scrape the contents of each can of sweetened condensed milk into small (1 quart/0.9 liter) zip-closure cooking pouches (one can per pouch), evacuate the air (page 11), and zip closed.

3. Submerge the pouches in the water oven and cook for 13 hours, removing the pouches to gently massage now and again during the cooking time.

4. Remove the pouches from the water bath and quick-chill them, submerged in ice water (half ice, half water) for 30 minutes.

5. Store the pouches in the refrigerator for up to 6 weeks. (Once opened, squeeze the remaining contents into a clean container with a tightly fitting lid and refrigerate to use for up to 6 weeks.)

Make the ice cream

1. Fill and preheat the water oven to 140°F (60°C).

2. In a bowl, beat the egg yolks with the sugar and non-fat dry milk until light yellow and thickened.

3. Scrape the seeds from the vanilla bean and add them and the half-and-half to the yolks and beat just enough to mix.

4. Pour the mixture into a large (1 gallon/3.8 liter) zip-closure cooking pouch, evacuate the air (page 11), and zip the seal closed.

5. Submerge the pouch in the water oven and cook for 45 minutes to 1 hour.

6. Remove the pouch from the water bath and quick chill it, submerged in ice water (half ice, half water) for 30 minutes. Refrigerate until ready to churn.

7. Churn the chilled mixture according to your ice cream machine's manufacturer's instructions.

8. Spoon into dishes, top with dulce de leche and a sprinkle of sea salt, and serve immediately. If a firmer consistency is desired, scoop the ice cream into a quart container, cover tightly, and freeze for one hour before serving.

For the dulce de leche
2 cans (14 oz/396 ml each) sweetened condensed milk

For the ice cream
6 large egg yolks
1 cup (6.5 oz/190 g) superfine (castor) sugar
1/4 cup (2 oz/60 ml) non-fat dry milk powder (organic if available)
1 quart (0.9 liter) half-and-half *
1/2 vanilla bean
Pinch of coarse sea salt

* For a lighter ice cream, substitute 3 cups (24 oz/710 ml) 2% milk plus 1 cup (8 oz/240 ml) light cream

gajar ka halwa (carrot pudding)

Courtesy of Chef Sam Hussain

Serves 4
Cooking time: 2 hours

1. Fill and preheat the water oven to 183°F (84°C).

2. Wash and grate the carrots.

3. Soak the nuts and raisins in water for 30 minutes.

4. In a large pouch put the shredded carrots, raisins, pistachios, almonds, and ghee and vacuum seal.

5. Submerge the pouch in the water oven to cook for 2 hours.

6. Meanwhile, in a saucepan over very low heat, warm the milk, stirring occasionally, for 1 hour.

7. Add the sugar, mix well, and cook until the sugar has dissolved and all the milk has been absorbed into the sugar.

8. Empty the contents of the cooked carrot pouch into the absorbed milk in the saucepan and mix well.

9. Add cardamom and stir for another 3 to 5 minutes.

10. Garnish with raisins, almonds, and pistachios.

11. Serve hot, room temperature, or cold.

2 pounds (1 kilo) carrots

2 tablespoons (30 ml) pistachios

2 tablespoons (30 ml) almonds

2 tablespoons (30 ml) raisins

2 tablespoons (30 ml) ghee (clarified butter)

36 ounces (1 liter) milk

2$\frac{1}{3}$ cups (16 oz/450 g) sugar (adjust to taste)

1 teaspoon (5 ml) cardamom seeds or powder

Additional raisins and nuts for garnish

chocolate zabaglione

8 large egg yolks

1 cup (7 oz/192 g) sugar

Pinch salt

$^1/_2$ cup (4 oz/120 ml) dry Marsala

$^1/_3$ cup (1 oz/30 g) unsweetened cocoa powder

$^1/_4$ cup (2 oz/60 ml) whipping cream or heavy cream

1 pound (0.9 kg) fresh strawberries, washed, hulled, and quartered

Serves 6
Cooking time: 20 minutes

1. Fill and preheat the water oven to 165°F (74°C).

2. Meanwhile, in a bowl, whisk together the egg yolks, sugar, salt and Marsala.

3. Add cocoa powder and whisk until completely combined, then add cream and whisk well.

4. Pour the mixture into a zip-seal cooking pouch, evacuate the air (page 11), and seal.

5. Submerge the pouch in the water oven to cook for 20 minutes, until thick and creamy.

6. Meanwhile, divide the strawberries among individual dessert bowls or stemmed cocktail glasses.

7. When ready to serve, pour the warm zabaglione over the strawberries, or if you prefer, pour the zabaglione into individual serving bowls, cover, and chill until set in the refrigerator, then garnish each bowl with a few fresh strawberries at serving.

pound cake with strawberries

Serves 8
Cooking time: 1 to 1½ hours

1. Fill the water oven just to the fill line, and preheat to 195°F (90.5°C).

2. Elevate the bottom perforated grill of the water oven about 2 inches (5 cm), either on a sous vide baking platform or non-rusting, adjustable wire rack for roasting.

3. Fill 2 mini-loaf pans or mini-Bundt pans with water and position them on the perforated grill to check water depth in the water oven. The water level in the bath should come no higher than to ½ inch (1.25 cm) below the rim of the baking pans.

4. Remove the pans, dry thoroughly, and spray with non-stick baking spray (cooking spray with flour). Set aside.

5. In a medium bowl, sift together the dry ingredients and set aside.

6. In a large bowl, beat the butter until it is creamed.

7. Add the sugar and continue to beat until the mixture is light and fluffy.

8. Add the cream cheese and lemon zest and beat again to mix thoroughly.

9. Beat in the eggs, one at a time.

10. Beat in half the flour followed by half the sour cream, then repeat with the remaining flour and sour cream.

11. Divide the batter between the baking pans, allowing a little room at the top.

12. Tear a sheet of aluminum foil about 12 inches (30 cm) long and fold it in half.

13. Position the filled baking pans on the elevated bottom grill and tent the foil over the baking pans to deflect any drips of condensation.

14. Cook in the water bath for 1 hour, and up to 90 minutes.

15. Remove the pans carefully from the water oven to a cooling rack. Cover lightly with a paper towel and let cool for 15 minutes.

16. Invert the pans to remove the cakes.

17. Slice and serve topped with fresh berries and mint, or a drizzle of dulce de leche (page 191), and whipped cream.

For the pound cake

¾ cup (3 oz/85 g) flour

1 teaspoon (5 ml) baking powder

¼ teaspoon (1.25 ml) salt

⅛ teaspoon (0.6 ml) baking soda

1 stick (4 oz/113g) butter, softened

1 cup (7 oz/204 g) sugar

1½ ounces (42 g) cream cheese, softened

1 lemon, for zest only

2 eggs, room temperature

½ cup (4 oz/120 ml) sour cream

For the berries

4 cups (21 oz/605 g) fresh strawberries, washed, stemmed, and quartered

½ cup (4 oz/120 ml) whipped cream, sweetened to your liking

8 sprigs fresh mint for garnish

chocolate pot de créme

Courtesy of Chef Jennifer Carden

Serves 4
Cooking time: 1 hour

1. Fill and preheat the water oven to 180°F (82°C).

2. Put the chocolate into a microwave-safe bowl and melt in the microwave on high, starting with 1 minute. Stir and continue melting in 30-second intervals, stirring well in between each, until just smooth.

3. In a medium heat-proof bowl, beat the egg yolks and sugar together and set aside.

4. On the stove top in a pan, heat the milk to a simmer, then slowly whisk a small amount of the hot milk into the egg mixture to temper the eggs.

5. Slowly pour the remaining hot milk into the egg mixture, while whisking.

6. Add the chocolate and whisk until smooth. Whisk in the cream and vanilla.

7. Put the mixture into a zip-seal cooking pouch, evacuate the air (page 11), and seal.

9. Submerge the pouch in the water bath to cook for 1 hour or until set.

Make the topping

10. Combine the tapioca and vinegar and set aside to marinate for 30 minutes.

11. In a bowl, whip the cream until it begins to thicken. Add the espresso powder and powdered sugar and continue to whip until stiff peaks form.

12. Divide the cooked créme among four ramekins or custard cups, and top each portion with whipped cream and a dollop of the balsamic tapioca.

5 ounces (142 g) semisweet chocolate, evenly chopped

3¹/₂ ounces (99 g) milk chocolate, evenly chopped

6 large egg yolks

¹/₂ cup (3.5 oz/100 g) brown sugar

¹/₂ cup (4 oz/120 ml) whole milk

2 cups (16 oz/473 ml) heavy cream

2 teaspoons (10 ml) pure vanilla extract

For the topping

¹/₂ cup (4 oz/120 ml) prepared tapioca (page 193)

¹/₈ cup (1 oz/30 ml) balsamic vinegar

¹/₂ cup (4 oz/120 ml) heavy cream

1 teaspoon (5 ml) instant espresso powder

2 tablespoons (30 ml) powdered sugar

almond custard sticky pudding

Serves 6 to 8
Cooking time: 1 ½ hours

1. Fill and preheat the water oven to 193°F (90°C).

2. In the bowl of an electric mixer fitted with the paddle attachment, mix the almond paste for about 2 minutes.

3. Add the butter and continue beating until blended, then beat in the sugar.

4. Add the eggs one at a time, beating until they are incorporated.

5. Remove the bowl from the mixer and fold in the flour.

6. Add the vanilla, almond extract, and salt.

7. Put the batter into a zip-seal cooking pouch, evacuate the air (page 11) and seal.

8. Put the pouch into the water oven and allow to cook for 90 minutes or until the pudding is firmly set.

9. Before serving, whip the cream, then when soft peaks form, add the almond extract and castor sugar and whip to firm peaks.

10. Spoon the warm pudding into dessert bowls and top with a dollop of the whipped cream and a few sliced almonds, if desired.

1 cup (8 oz/220 g) almond paste

2 sticks (8 oz/220 g) butter

1 cup (7 oz/200 g) sugar

4 eggs

1 cup (4 oz/113 g) sifted cake flour

1 tablespoon (15 ml) vanilla extract

$1/4$ teaspoon (1.25 ml) almond extract

$1/2$ teaspoon (2.5 ml) salt

For the topping

$1/2$ cup (4 oz/120 ml) heavy whipping cream

$1/8$ teaspoon (0.625 ml) almond extract

$1/4$ cup (8 oz/220 g) superfine (castor) sugar

Sliced almonds for garnish

ruby red velvet cake

Courtesy of Susie Norris

Serves 9 to 12
Cooking time: 1½ hours

1. Fill the water oven just to the fill line, and preheat to 190°F (88°C).

2. Elevate the bottom perforated grill of the water oven about 2 inches (5 cm), either on a sous vide baking platform or non-rusting, adjustable wire rack for roasting.

3. Fill 3 mini-loaf pans or mini-Bundt pans with water and position them on the perforated grill to check water depth in the water oven. The water level in the bath should come no higher than to ½ inch (1.25 cm) below the rim of the baking pans.

4. Prepare 3 mini loaf pans or mini Bundt pans by spraying them with non-stick baking spray (cooking spray with flour).

5. In a bowl, combine flour, cocoa powder, and salt and set aside.

6. In a separate bowl, cream butter and sugar together until it becomes light and fluffy.

7. Add the egg to the butter/sugar mixture.

8. Add the puréed beets, melted chocolate, and vanilla to the butter/sugar mixture.

9. In a separate medium-size bowl, blend the sour cream and buttermilk together.

10. Then to the beet mixture, alternate additions of the flour mixture and buttermilk mixture in thirds until both are mixed into the batter.

11. Finally, put the baking soda in a separate small bowl and add the vinegar. (It will foam up.) Fold the soda and vinegar mixture into the cake batter.

12. Mix in a few drops of red food coloring, if desired, and pour the batter into the prepared pans.

13. Carefully position the pans on the baking rack, ensuring that the water level comes no higher than within ½ inch (1.27 cm) of the rim.

14. Tent a piece of aluminum foil over the pans to divert any drips of condensate from the lid of the machine.

1⅛ cups (4 oz/113 g) cake flour

1½ tablespoons (22.5 ml) cocoa powder (preferably natural or non-alkalised)

½ teaspoon (2.5 ml) salt

6 tablespoons (90 ml) butter, at room temperature

¾ cups (5 oz/144 g) sugar

1 egg

¼ cup (1.5 oz/42 g) beet purée

2 ounces (60 g) melted bittersweet chocolate

1½ teaspoons (7.5 ml) vanilla

¼ cup (1 oz/30 g) sour cream

¼ cup (2 oz/60 ml) buttermilk

½ teaspoon (2.5 ml) baking soda

1½ teaspoons (7.5 ml) white vinegar

Red food coloring (optional)

For the chocolate glaze

8 ounces (220 g) milk chocolate, finely chopped

¼ cup (2 oz/60 g) unsalted butter

2 tablespoons (30 ml) milk

1 tablespoon (15 ml) light corn syrup

1 teaspoon (5 ml) kosher salt

ruby red
velvet cake

continued from page 203

15. Cook for approximately 90 minutes or until the cake is fully set.

16. Remove the pans from the water oven and allow them to cool until they are room temperature.

Make the glaze

1. Add 2 cups of ice to the water bath and reset the temperature to 176°F (80°C).

2. Combine all of the glaze ingredients in a zip-seal cooking pouch, evacuate the air (page 11), and seal.

3. Submerge the pouch in the water oven and cook until the ingredients have melted, about 20 minutes.

4. Remove the pouch, knead the contents to thoroughly blend, and return to the water bath for another 10 to 15 minutes.

5. When ready to serve, release the cakes from the pans.

6. Remove the glaze pouch from the water oven, dry the exterior, snip one corner, and drizzle the warm glaze generously over the cakes.

winter fruits in spiced wine

Courtesy of Chef Raymond Blanc

Serves 4
Cooking time: 1 hour

1. Fill and preheat the water oven to 185°F (85°C).

2. Make the vanilla syrup by boiling the water and castor sugar until the sugar has dissolved. Roughly chop the vanilla pods, removing the hard nib at one end, and purée together with the sugar water.

3. Make the red wine jus by boiling the red wine in a large sauté pan over high heat for approximately 1 minute to remove the alcohol.

4. Add the water and all the other wine jus ingredients, bring to a gentle simmer for 5 minutes, and leave to cool.

5. Put all the fruit ingredients into a zip-seal cooking pouch and add the wine jus. Evacuate the air from the pouch (page 11) and seal.

6. Submerge the pouch in the water oven and cook for 40 minutes.

7. Remove the pouch from the water bath and allow to cool to room temperature, or chill in the refrigerator for 1 hour, before serving.

8. Arrange all the fruits, spices, red wine and cooking juices in a large dish, and serve.

Variations: Freeze some of the cooking liquor to create delicate flakes of iced spiced wine by scraping with a fork. Serve either on top of the chilled fruits or as a little pre-dessert treat in a small shot glass.

1 quince, peeled, cored, and cut into 8 segments

$1/4$ pineapple, peeled, trimmed, and quartered

1 sweet apple (Cox, Gala, or similar) peeled, cored, and quartered

1 pear (Williams or similar) peeled, cored, and quartered

4 Agen prunes (optional)

For the red wine jus

$6^{1}/_{4}$ ounces (185 ml) red wine, such as Cabernet Sauvignon*

$6^{1}/_{4}$ ounces (185 ml) water

4 tablespoons (60 ml) castor sugar

1 teaspoon (5 ml) vanilla syrup

$1/2$ cinnamon stick

1 pinch black pepper

2 bay leaves

2 cloves

2 lemon slices $1/4$-inch (1-mm) thick

2 orange slices $1/4$-inch (1-mm) thick

For the vanilla syrup

$3/4$ cup (6 oz/180 ml) water

$3/4$ cup (6 oz/169 g) castor sugar

6 large vanilla pods

* Choose an inexpensive, deep, rich-colored cabernet or merlot. Pinot noir are too light and delicate for this recipe.

contributors

Douglas Baldwin (14, 127) wrote the world-renowned *A Practical Guide to Sous Vide Cooking*, which has been translated into three languages, and *Sous Vide for the Home Cook*. He is an applied mathematician by profession, and researches nonlinear wave phenomena at the University of Colorado at Boulder. (douglasbaldwin.com)

Rex Bird (128) is Chief Operating Officer for Eades Appliance Technology, makers of the SousVide Supreme water oven.

Richard Blais (121, 174, 177, 178) is an American chef, reality show contestant, restaurateur and author. He was the runner-up of the fourth season of the reality television show *Top Chef* and the winner of season eight, *Top Chef: All-Stars*. He owns and operates Trail Blais, that has consulted on, designed, and operated multiple outposts of Flip Burger Boutique, HD1, and The Spence. (richardblais.net)

Raymond Blanc OBE (47, 205) is one of Britain's most respected chefs. Blanc is the owner and chef at Le Manoir aux Quat' Saisons, a hotel-restaurant in Great Milton, Oxfordshire, England. The restaurant has two Michelin stars and scored 9/10 in the *Good Food Guide*. He is entirely self-taught. (raymondblanc.com)

Jennifer Carden (200) is a chef, food stylist, and cookbook author. She wrote *Toddler Café: Fast Recipes and Fun Ways to Feed Even the Pickiest Eater*, and her husband, photographer Matthew Carden, took the pictures. She has worked on books by Mollie Katzen and Jacques Pepin and has done live television food styling for Guy Fieri of Guy's Big Bite. (thetoddlercafe.blogspot.com)

Katherine Emmenegger, C.C.C., (71, 77, 79, 85) is Executive Chef at Great News! Cooking School in Pacific Beach, California. (great-news.com)

Phillip Foss (93, 163) is the chef and owner of EL Ideas which, in its first year, was awarded three stars by the *Chicago Tribune*, named "Best New Restaurant" in

Chicago Magazine, and won Chicago reader's "Favorite Restaurant of 2011." (twitter.com/phillipfoss)

Sharone Hakman (69, 72), is a chef and owner of a barbecue sauce company. Formerly a financial planner, he left the corporate world to follow his true love for food by pursuing a career as a chef, and appeared on Fox television's hit show *Master Chef*. (sharonehakman.com)

Sean Heather (155) launched his first Gastown restaurant, The Irish Heather, in 1997 in Vancouver, B.C., and has since expanded his Heather Hospitality Group empire to 10 restaurants, including the Salt Tasting Room, Bitter Tasting Room, Judas Goat Taberna, and Ranier Provisions. In 2013 he was inducted into the B.C. Restaurant Hall of Fame.

Josh Horrigan (46, 149, 159) is a chef and Director of Industry Relations at The Chef's Academy in Indianapolis, Indiana. (thechefsacademy.com)

Sam Hussain (91, 133, 192, 193, 196) is chef and owner of Cafe Rickshaw, a restaurant in Wolverhampton, U.K., featuring modern Indian cuisine. (caferickshaw.com)

Stephane Lemangnen (156) is a private chef, food blogger, and former restaurant owner in New York City. (zencancook.com)

John Loydall (97), photographer and food blogger, lives and works in the U.K. (food.johnloydall.co.uk)

Sally MacColl (57, 119) is a food blogger and passionate cook who develops sous vide recipes and techniques for home cooks. (svkitchen.com)

Brian McCracken and **Dana Tough** (22, 23, 25, 27, 29, 30, 31, 33) have been named in the nation's Top Five Chefs (by Gayot) as Rising Star Chefs and were nominated by the editors of *Food & Wine* magazine for "The Peoples Best New Chef" awards. Tavern Law, their Prohibition-era inspired cocktail bar in Seattle,

Washington, was named by *GQ* magazine as one of the Best 25 Bars in America. (mccrackentough.com)

Vicky McDonald (189) writes a food recipe blog where she shares her thoughts on cooking, eating, foodie finds, and gadgets. (stasty.com)

Pam McKinstry (39, 105, 117, 131, 135) is the author of four *Sconset Cafe* cookbooks and two books on organic cooking, *Food to Live By* and *The Earthbound Cook*. She lives in Carmel, California, where she develops sous vide recipes and writes a food blog. (svkitchen.com)

Susie Norris (203) is a cookbook author, artisan chocolatier, pastry chef/instructor and educational fundraiser. Her cookbook, *Chocolate Bliss*, was released by Random House/Celestial Arts in November 2009, and *Hand-Crafted Candy Bars* was released by Chronicle Books in March 2013.

Ivaylo Peshev (21) is a mixologist and bartender at Trattoria Vittoria in Santa Barbara, California.

Vivian Peterson (114) is an Executive Chef and former restaurant owner who teaches sous vide cooking classes in Seattle, Washington.

Lenard Rubin (151) was inducted in 2002 into the Arizona Culinary Hall of Fame and in 2006 was chosen "Chef of the Year" for the Phoenix, Arizona area by the American Culinary Federation Chefs' Association of Greater Phoenix. He is a two-time James Beard House invitee with 25 years experience as a chef, most notably with the Ritz-Carlton hotel chain and as chef/partner at The Vig and The Vig Uptown.

Heath Schecter (129, 143, 145) has worked in the restaurant industry for over 25 years in Chicago, Wisconsin and Arizona. He currently works as a chef in research and development, specializing in sauces.

Alex Seidel (37, 167) has been recognized by the James Beard Foundation with several nominations for "Best Chef Southwest." *Food and Wine* magazine named him as 2010's "Best New Chef." Fruition, his restaurant in Denver, Colorado, serves a menu based on locally-sourced, primarily from Seidel's Verde Farms, in Larkspur, Colorado. (fruitionrestaurant.com)

Michael Solomonov (61, 183) is co-owner of the Israeli restaurant Zahav in Philadelphia, Pennsylvania, and Cook + Solo restaurant group. He won the James Beard "Best Chef: Mid-Atlantic" award in 2011. (zahavrestaurant.com)

Stephanie Stiavetti (58) is a food blogger, cookbook author, culinary media consultant, and writer for NPR, Serious Eats, The Huffington Post, and KQED. (theculinarylife.com)

Michael Vetsch (43) is Executive Chef at Uncorked Wine Bar in Snoqualmie, Washington. (uncorked-wine.com)

Nathan Weber (22, 29, 30, 33) developed sous vide cocktail recipes working with infusions by Chefs Brian McCracken and Dana Tough at Tavern Law in Seattle, Washington.

Jason Wilson (137, 144, 161) was declared one of the Top Ten New Chefs in North America in 2006 by the prestigious *Food and Wine* magazine, and in 2010 won the James Beard Award for "Best Chef: Northwest." He is chef and owner of CRUSH in Seattle, Washington. (chefjasonwilson.com)

Jamie Watson (157) trained at the French Culinary Institute in New York. He lives and works in Nashville, Tennessee, where he owns and operates two restaurants. In 2013 he was named one of "Best Chefs America." (chefjamiewatson.com)

index

216

ISBN: 978-0-9844936-1-6

Printed in China

1 2 3 4 5 6 7 8 9 10

Book design by Faith Keating

Paradox Press